LEADERS' JOURNAL

40 days of self-coaching

John D.H. Greenway
Andy Blacknell
Andy Coombe

Leaders' Journal

40 days of self-coaching

Contents

Section A
Introduction   **1**

1. Purpose   3
2. The Leader's Journey   7
3. Pivotal Moments   16
4. Get the most from Leaders' Journal   20

Section B
40 Days   **23**

Week 1   You
DAY 1	Grand Slam	*Leaders are teachable*	26
DAY 2	The Mandela Challenge	*Your beliefs govern your choices*	28
DAY 3	Best cards	*Be brilliant at who you are!*	30
DAY 4	34.2% salinity	*Adopt the role of Chief Refresher*	32
DAY 5	The chart table	*Agility is a key leader behaviour*	34

Week 2   Your People
DAY 6	Livid	*Find the right people*	38
DAY 7	The twist	*Use your people's talent – or lose it.*	40
DAY 8	Valentines	*Appreciate your people*	42
DAY 9	Italian baked pie	*Build your people's confidence*	44
DAY 10	Terrible news	*Do the vision*	46

Week 3   See the big picture
DAY 11	The stumbling man	*Keep your eyes wide open*	50
DAY 12	A to B	*See the connections you need to make*	52
DAY 13	CMRM	*Think outside-in*	54
DAY 14	Gorillas	*Look inside the box*	56
DAY 15	Tipperary	*See the here and now*	58

Week 4 Choose the right direction

DAY 16	Debt-free	*Understand the Why*	62
DAY 17	Too broke to manage	*Prioritise your priorities*	64
DAY 18	Chicago	*Choose your golden rules*	66
DAY 19	Icelandic waiters	*Set the right expectations*	68
DAY 20	What's your ding?	*Choose your choices*	70

Week 5 Do the right things

DAY 21	The scrapbook	*Look to be transformative*	74
DAY 22	A hundred parakeets	*Let your creative juices flow*	76
DAY 23	Usain Bolt	*Being proactive means being first*	78
DAY 24	683,806 hours	*Be productive - work smart and hard*	80
DAY 25	Just 15 minutes	*Be prepared to say 'No'*	82

Week 6 Check progress

DAY 26	The merchant of death	*Seek honest feedback*	86
DAY 27	The elephant	*Face up to reality*	88
DAY 28	Easy lunch	*Adapt or die*	90
DAY 29	The Santa Monica warehouse	*Appreciate your assets*	92
DAY 30	The paperweight	*Communicate the change*	94

Week 7 Be inspired

DAY 31	Little chance of making money	*Follow your ideas*	98
DAY 32	In memory of Doris	*Be an inspiration*	100
DAY 33	Mud airstrips	*Actions communicate and engage others*	102
DAY 34	There is no mistake	*Leadership is 24/7*	104
DAY 35	The chauffeur	*Try something new*	106

Week 8 Your life

DAY 36	Ebola	*Follow your calling*	110
DAY 37	The titanic mistake	*A life of integrity is unsinkable*	112
DAY 38	Rain or snow	*Put first things first*	114
DAY 39	Buried in the rubble	*Leave the legacy you want*	116
DAY 40	10,000 ways that won't work	*Keep on going*	118

Section C:
The Really Useful Appendix   **121**

SOAP: Strategy-on-a-Page   123
Assess your approach to navigate as a leader   125
DAY 1   *The GROW model*   126
DAY 2   *The Four Circles*   127
DAY 3   *What are your best cards?*   128
DAY 4   *Greek Temple model of leadership*   129
DAY 5   *Daniel Goleman – Leadership Styles*   130
DAY 6   *Hiring for success*   131
DAY 7   *Different strokes for different folks*   132
DAY 8   *Engaging your people*   133
DAY 9   *Boosting confidence*   134
DAY 10   *Patrick Lencioni – The Five Dysfunctions of a Team*   135
DAY 11   *Clarity and Confidence*   136
DAY 12   *Your solar system*   137
DAY 13   *The "Trusted Adviser"*   138
DAY 14   *Co-consultancy*   139
DAY 15   *The Big Health Check*   140
DAY 16   *Simon Sinek – The Golden Circle*   141
DAY 17   *The Eisenhower Matrix*   142
DAY 18   *Know your values*   143
DAY 19   *Ask great questions*   144
DAY 20   *The wisdom of Steve Jobs*   145
DAY 21   *Make transformative choices*   147
DAY 22   *Be creative*   148
DAY 23   *Be proactive*   149
DAY 24   *Be productive*   150
DAY 25   *Be reactive only when you need to*   151
DAY 26   *Listening*   152
DAY 27   *Face the facts*   153
DAY 28   *Bruce Tuckman - Stages of team development*   154

DAY 29   *Belbin - Team Roles*   155

DAY 30   *John Kotter – Leading change*   156

DAY 31   *Brick and Blanket test*   157

DAY 32   *Derek Sivers - How to start a movement*   158

DAY 33   *Transactional Analysis*   159

DAY 34   *What really motivates us?*   160

DAY 35   *Appetite for risk*   161

DAY 36   *The Life Direction Wheel: Core Vision, Values and Goals*   163

DAY 37   *The Life Direction Wheel: Private*   164

DAY 38   *The Life Direction Wheel: Public*   165

DAY 39   *The Life Direction Wheel: Professional*   166

DAY 40   *Congratulations…*   167

Thanks   168

Section A
Introduction

"To forget one's purpose is the commonest form of stupidity."

Friedrich Nietzsche

1. Purpose

"He just threw my Christmas present into the fire!"

Every Christmas morning we would drive 200 miles from my in-laws to my parents. The car would be jam packed with kids, cases and presents.

This particular year I had decided to buy cherry trees as presents for my parents and two sisters. It would have been impossible to put them in the car; so I hatched a plan.

I called each of them individually and asked for their help. Each conversation went along the same lines.

"Could you please buy a cherry tree for *abc* and I will pay you? Let's keep it a big secret from them. Please hide the tree in *xyz* and I will pick it up on Christmas Day."

They each really enjoyed being part of the plot.

When we arrived on Christmas morning I found the three cherry trees in the three locations that we had agreed. But I was shocked.

I had expected to see eight-foot cherry saplings in substantial pots. Instead I found eight-inch shoots in three small flower pots. This was a disaster. What pathetic looking Christmas presents — and I had paid very good money for them.

To avoid a total anti-climax I decided to arrange a treasure hunt for the tiny cherry trees. At least, we could make it fun even if the presents might be seen as low-budget.

All the family joined in too and discovered their respective trees in the pots. But as my brother-in-law brought one pot into the house he uprooted the little tree and threw it into the fire, saying "What a pathetic present!"

I couldn't believe it: "He just threw my Christmas present into the fire!"

At the very same time my nephew appeared at the window, with a big smile on his face, carrying three eight-foot cherry saplings.

It turned out that I was the one who been hoodwinked.

It had started so well. They had been willing secret collaborators with me, but a big coincidence had happened. Although they lived 25 miles apart they had ordered the trees from the very same garden centre. That may not have been a show stopper, but they also turned up at the very same time to collect the trees.

They asked other, "What are you doing here?" Once they realised what was happening they started to plot together.

They decided to put a small twig in each plant pot and hide the real trees elsewhere. I was well and truly caught out.

The good news is, however, there have been three great crops of cherries every year since.

Maybe this is an unusual way to introduce a book on leadership, but there are some lessons and parallels for *Leaders' Journal*:

- This book is about growth and reaping the benefits over many years to come.

- It is also a gift – even if you have paid for it. We are sharing the best we have, and we hope that you can use it to your benefit.

- *Leaders' Journal* has many other short stories which we hope will "paint a picture" to get a point across.

- Because it is best read over 40 days, things will conspire to put you off following through. We encourage you - it will be worth persevering.

- Finally, we hope that you will enjoy it. Humour is an important part of leadership.

Moving on to leadership

Leadership is seriously important, dynamic and challenging.

It is seriously important because it's core to the results and success - or failure - of every enterprise.

It is dynamic because it's characterised by constant change.

It is challenging because it requires effort, determination and perseverance.

Do you have someone to help you on your journey? Perhaps a coach or mentor who is helping you grow personally and think through the challenges and plans you have? Although we would suggest nothing is as good as a face-to-face meeting with a trusted adviser, this book is possibly the next best thing. It's designed to support a mentor relationship or to help you coach yourself.

We have written this book with three things in mind:

- Leadership is about taking people with you on a journey of common purpose and direction

- The journey will be unpredictable … more akin to navigating choppy seas than driving along a straight road.

- We want to help you navigate your voyage more effectively and reach your chosen destinations.

This book is a sequel to *Leaders' Map*.

Leaders' Map provides a practical framework for any and every leadership journey. We recommend that you read it first, but it's not essential. You could read it in an hour and a half and use it as an on-going reference point.

40 days

Leaders' Journal should not, however, be read in 90 minutes. It's intended to be consumed over the next 40 days or so. We don't want you to get indigestion.

40 days is an interesting time span. Things can change over 40 days. Mind-sets can be re-set, purpose and direction can become clearer, confidence can be strengthened and new habits may be formed. We are told that Jesus spent 40 days fasting, preparing for his career change from carpenter to teacher.

To make this work, we would recommend that you mentally sign up for the next eight weeks. There's little point in consuming all the tablets in one go. It's a daily regime.

Leaders' Journal is your daily journal for the next eight weeks. That's why there are 40 fairly empty pages in this book – for your personal reflections and jottings.

Each week there are five short daily readings and the journal for you to complete.

In the Really Useful Appendix (starting on page 121) there is a range of great practical ideas and tools - one for each day. If we haven't created the tools or generated the ideas ourselves, we have attributed the original authors to the best of our knowledge.

This is intentionally called a journal and not a manual. Manuals are great for predictable procedures, journals are better for capturing the story of a dynamic journey.

Jon Bon Jovi wrote: "Map out your future, but do it in pencil".

Find a good pencil (and an eraser) as you read this book. There will be plenty of opportunity to think, clarify, trial, do, review, learn. You will want to keep a record.

We hope that all the ideas we present will be thought-provoking, that many will be practically useful to you, that some will be inspirational and that maybe one or two will even be transformational. Challenge yourself - it's what you take away, try, apply and then embed into your leadership armoury that is most important.

Commit ten minutes each day to sharpening and shaping up as a leader. The two spare days each week give you time to go into more depth on a topic or to just "go fishin'".

Complete your journal each day. Commit your reflections and "takeaways" to writing. Record your intentions to act. Let your journal be a daily provocation and reminder to you.

This is your book, your journal. It is personal. You could increase the value by going through the eight-week programme with a "coaching buddy". Meet each week to compare notes and provide a level of challenge and accountability. You could take it further by inviting all of your team to participate. The benefits could be multiplied - it may be the best team-building initiative that you ever undertake.

We hope that this book will make a big difference to you and to those you will be serving in the future.

P.S. We have used a number of personal anecdotes to illustrate our points. If you try to stitch the stories together, they won't fit - that's because we are three authors!

"Change is inevitable - except from a vending machine."
Robert C. Gallagher

2. The Leader's Journey

Many business planning meetings go something like this: "We are here and we want to get there," as the speaker boldly draws a straight line from the bottom left to the top right on the flip chart.

Unfortunately for all the times that we have seen this drawn, we have never once seen it work out like that.

Yes, the Trans-Australian Railway has a 478 kilometre dead straight track between Ooldea and Loongana. Yes, the ancient Romans built the straight 53 kilometre Ermine Street in England. But life doesn't go in a straight line. We do not have total control and our path is far from being obstacle-free. We live in a highly changing, dynamic world. Our 21st century environment has been described as a "VUCA world" - volatile, uncertain, complex and ambiguous.

Road or rail maps are not the best ways to look at leadership. The real world has changing weather conditions, choppy waters and unexpected obstacles. The real leadership journey that you face is much more like sailing the seas than cruising along an empty motorway.

Leadership is the art of navigating, through all weathers and conditions, to achieve your purpose and mission. Unfortunately, when sailing, there are no signposts in the water that say turn right or left. Your biggest leadership challenge will be how you navigate ... rather than how you steer. Navigation requires judgement and not just following a pre-ordained path.

WE TRY TO GET
FROM A TO B
IN A STRAIGHT LINE

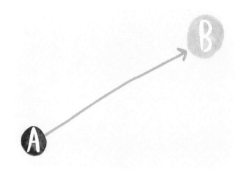

...BUT LIFE IS UNPREDICTABLE & CIRCUMSTANCES CHANGE

WINDS BLOW... WAVES RISE...
CURRENTS PULL...
OBSTACLES BLOCK &
OPPORTUNITIES ARISE

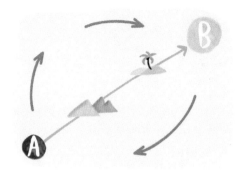

OUR JOURNEY IS MORE LIKE SAILING THAN DRIVING
ALONG A STRAIGHT ROAD

WE HAVE TO NAVIGATE
THROUGH CIRCUMSTANCES
TOWARDS OUR
ASPIRATIONS

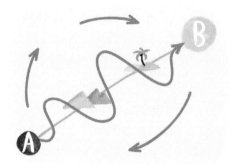

Your own map

Let's get practical and start thinking about you as a leader and creating your own leaders' map

You may be running a business, heading up part of an organisation, leading a team or managing a project… or just be "captain of your own boat". Either way, tackle the following question head on:

What is your big vision, your crazy hope, your all-consuming aspiration? Vision is a picture of the future that stirs you.

In the words of the Spice Girls, "What do you want ... really, really want?" For example you might say, "To become the best retail service in town" or "To get our product in every home" or "Education for all in Africa".

It should be something big, something audacious, something that inspires and pulls you. You should be able to see it in your mind's eye.

Make it short and memorable. Make it tweetable. Get your pencil out and write it in less than 140 characters in the vision cloud.

The great connectors

Now let's move on and think about the things that will connect everything together for you. They are called "values".

They connect where you are to where you want to get to. They are like the shaft of the arrow, connecting the bottom left (on your diagram) to the top right. Without the shaft, the arrow can't fly.

You could describe your values as your "golden rules". Make them pithy and memorable like, "Customer comes first" or "Think different, do different" or "Care for colleagues". They should reflect what you really believe in and not just some wishful thinking. John Stuart Mill said "One person with a belief is equal to

99 who have only interests."

What are your top three values, your bedrock beliefs, your golden rules?

Just check that they reflect both you and reality. It shouldn't be something wishy-washy or pie in the sky. Once you're happy with them, write them down next to the arrow shaft.

Okay, now what would success look like?

Leadership is about aiming for and achieving tangible results; results that are aligned to your vision.

Michelangelo said: "The greatest danger for most of us is not that our aim is too high and we miss it, but that it is too low and we reach it."

Dilbert – cartoon hero of the well-known satirical comic strip about office life - said: "Aim low, reach your goals and avoid disappointment."

Setting the aim is important. As a leader you set the expectations - it is your responsibility. It's your choice. It is also a skill. Spend some time over the next eight weeks thinking about it and refining your ability to set the right aims and expectations.

What are your goals? What results do you want? These should not be fluffy, but have a pointy end. Make them specific so you can measure whether you have achieved them. For example "Win the league" or "Smile ten times a day" or

"Make a 20% profit".

What are your top three goals?

Re-check that they are in line with your vision. Write them down next to the arrow head.

Don't worry if you are finding this difficult or if you think that you haven't got it quite right. We've done this exercise hundreds of times with executives and seven out of ten find it surprisingly tough. The important thing is that you are beginning to distil and crystallise your thinking. If it isn't clear in your mind you can't make it clear to somebody else.

Albert Einstein said: "Everything should be made as simple as possible, but not simpler."

Changing realities

Your *vision, values* and *goals* should be the things that are enduring, irrespective of your changing, unpredictable environment. So let's set them within the real context of your role.

What are the winds, waves and currents in your environment?

What lies ahead on your route? What are the jagged rocks jutting out of the jasper sea or what is the palm-laden desert island?

Which ones are *risks* and which ones are *opportunities*?

Winston Churchill said, "A pessimist sees the difficulty in every opportunity; an optimist sees the opportunity in every difficulty".

If they are opportunities they will help you to progress on your journey. If they are risks they may hold you back.

Think broadly, look widely. What are the top three things that could be opportunities? Opportunities come in very different ways. A sports manager may want to buy a new player, a retailer may see the gap in the market to buy a new store or an executive may want to develop her skills by investing in a personal mentor.

What are the top three opportunities in your environment?
1.
2.
3.

Some of those waves and currents may hinder progress. The jagged rocks could sink you. You have to be alert to risks.

Losing top players from that sports team could really hit results and the league position. Bad weather could hit footfall and profits for the store's critical winter season. Staff problems in the factory could distract the executive from investing in developing the leadership skills that would have prevented the problems in the first place.

What are the top two risks for you and your enterprise?
1.
2.

Be realistic and practical

Let's get real.

Where are you now? And - as President Bartlet says in the drama *The West Wing* – "What's next?"

Your *current position* should describe your present coordinates – where are you on the journey? This should be in relation to the goals that you have set for yourself. So in relation to the goals that you set above, your *current position* may be "8th in the league" or "smiling twice a day" or "3% profit". Be brutally honest. Don't kid yourself.

Next steps is the section that connects *current position* to your *vision, values* and goals. What must you do to progress in the right direction? These should be medium-term steps that will take you towards your longer-term destination.

Some examples may be: search for a new defence coach, win five more customers, reduce electricity bills, or hire a more successful and amusing sales and marketing director who will make you smile more.

Your daily and weekly to-do lists should then address your medium-term *next steps*.

Complete the map and pull it all together into one view on a page. This will enable you to tell your leadership story very simply, building step-by-step, just with a pencil and paper. It is a powerful way to engage others and literally draw them in.

Here is a reminder of our definitions:

Vision - what is your big aspiration?

Values - what are your golden rules?

Goals - what are your longer term objectives? What will success look like?

Current position - where are you now on the journey?

Opportunities - what will help you to progress?

Risks - what may hold you back?

Next steps - what are your mid-term priorities?

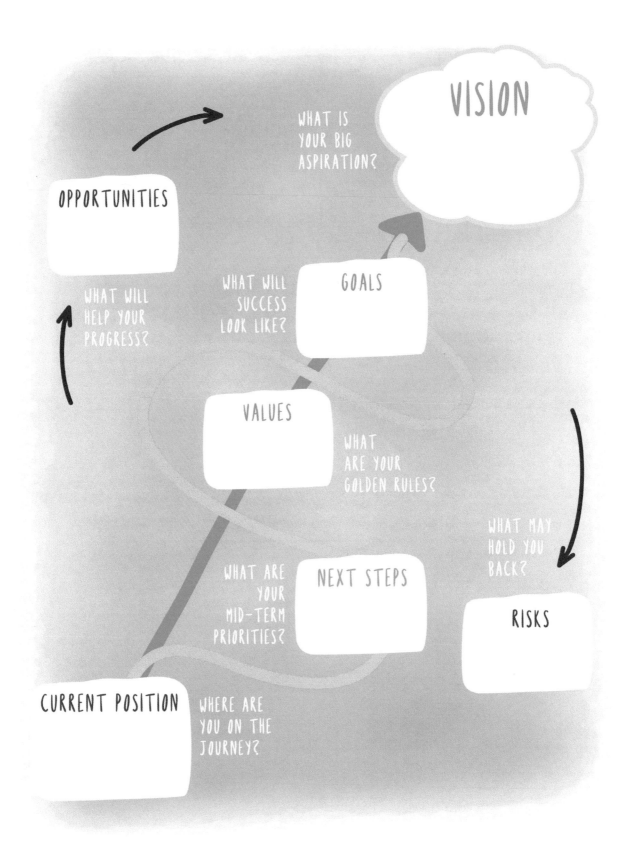

VISION

WHAT IS
YOUR BIG
ASPIRATION?

OPPORTUNITIES

WHAT WILL
HELP YOUR
PROGRESS?

WHAT WILL
SUCCESS
LOOK LIKE?

GOALS

VALUES

WHAT
ARE YOUR
GOLDEN RULES?

WHAT MAY
HOLD YOU
BACK?

WHAT ARE
YOUR
MID-TERM
PRIORITIES?

NEXT STEPS

RISKS

CURRENT POSITION

WHERE ARE
YOU ON THE
JOURNEY?

Now that you have just completed your map it is worth reflecting on the words of a five-star general who later became the 34th US President, Dwight D. Eisenhower: "Plans are nothing; planning is everything."

As the architect of the D-Day landings he knew a thing or two about plans and planning. Plans are static, planning is active.

The above is planning and not plans. It is your storyboard of the future that you can share with others, safe in the knowledge that circumstances will change. We have factored that in.

Remember that your *vision, values* and *goals* are your constants. They help you to chart your course; everything else will change. Therefore over the next eight weeks expect change. It is a good job you used a pencil and not a pen. (You did, didn't you?)

P.S. We have included a SoaP - Strategy on a Page - as the first tool in the Really Useful Appendix (see page 123). It provides an alternative format to capture your overview.

"To finish the moment, to find the journey's end in every step of the road, to live the greatest number of good hours, is wisdom … Since our office is with moments, let us husband them."

Ralph Waldo Emerson

3. Pivotal Moments

What do you think are the ten most important pivotal moments in history?

Would you include Hammurabi issuing his Code of Law in 1750 BC or Michelangelo accepting a commission to paint the Sistine Chapel in 1508 or Louis Pasteur curing a child of rabies in 1885?

They are all mentioned in lists that we researched. If you are a lawyer you may have chosen Hammurabi, or an art critic could have highlighted Michelangelo or a medic might have gone for Louis Pasteur because these were pivotal moments in each of their respective fields.

The thesaurus uses other words to describe a pivotal moment: critical point, crossroad, defining moment, crucial occurrence, turning point, change, moment of truth.

The Greek word "kairos" gives us another perspective.

The ancient Greeks had two words for "time". Their word "chronos" (from which we get our word "chronology") described *quantity* of time – minutes, hours, days. They used a second word, however, to describe *quality* of time: "kairos".

Kairos is about a time of change, a time of opportunity, a significant moment when nothing will be the same again, dividing the past from the future, when the divine invades the mundane and life is changed.

What have been the kairos moments or pivotal moments in your life?

What made them pivotal moments?

There was a turning of some sort. Life was going in one direction before and now it is going in another. Just like a boat tacking or jibing at sea. The wind was blowing in a certain direction but like a sailor you decided to turn. Events happened around you but you or somebody responded to the event in a particular way and things changed.

Usually we would describe pivotal moments as events of major significance. We may assume them to be rare.

When Neil Armstrong first put his foot on the moon's surface on 21st July 1969 it was a pivotal moment in space exploration and a "giant leap for mankind". Actually it was just an extension of many smaller, daily pivotal moments that led to that "one small step for man".

We can all look back and spot a pivotal moment. On occasions we can even spot a pivotal moment as it is occurring. We recognise that we are involved in a significant change. It is much more difficult to anticipate pivotal moments, but that is what we are going to try to do each day over the next eight weeks.

Each day identify a potential pivotal moment (only looking back will you be able to figure out what was actually the pivotal moment of the day).You might choose a meeting with a client, a difficult discussion with a team member whom you want to help turn around or even some "kairos" time with one of your children or a friend.

The point is that you will give it special, conscious attention. It will enable you to be highly mindful and be intentional. You can visualise and anticipate what you want to achieve and how you want to make "a turning for the better". On your journal page there will be space for you to anticipate *one* pivotal moment each day, to describe how you want to tackle it and to record the outcome.

This will be a unique opportunity for you to record *40 pivotal moments* and to practise your turning, your tacking and jibing.

You will be choosing to make the moments pivotal. They may be big or small events – it is your choice. Sometimes you will succeed, other times you might fail, but always you will be stretching and learning. It is all part of learning to navigate more effectively as a leader.

Navigational principles

In *Leaders' Map* we identified five key navigational principles. Each one is important in its own right, but together they will help you to make the turns you need to make when you are at the helm.

They start with five verbs or "doing words": SEE; CHOOSE; DO; CHECK; BE.

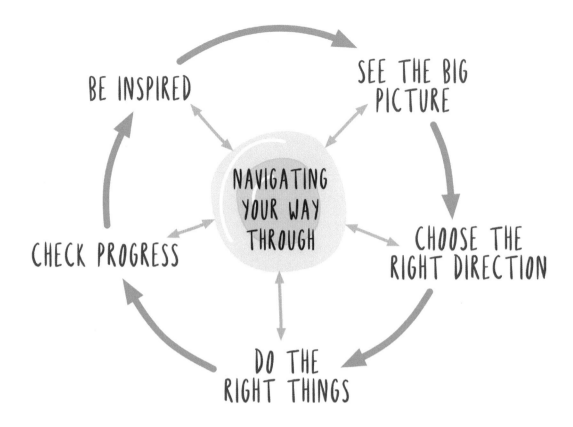

As you continue your journey they will be helpful prompts.

- Am I aware of the bigger picture? Is my vision clear? What is the weather forecast?

- Have we got clear goals? Are we heading in the right direction? Are my people aware why we have taken this turn?

- What are my priorities today? How can I be more proactive? How can I use my time more effectively?

- Let's be realistic with the progress that we are making. Are we learning from our mistakes? Have we celebrated our victories?

- What inspires me? How do I keep up my own motivation? How am I enabling others to grow and thrive?

These five principles form the spine of the 40-day self-coaching journal. These are daily principles. During Weeks 3-7 you will be "unpacking" each one and learning how to apply them to your daily situations.

Leaders' Journal is not intended to be prescriptive. We are sharing principles and ideas that we have seen work in diverse business settings. It's your call which ones you pick up and how you run with them.

Leaders wear "L" plates: "L" for learning

We wouldn't dare claim that we have mastered the ideas and behaviours mentioned in these pages. We, like you, are "work in progress". An important aim of *Leaders' Journal*, however, is to provoke and create opportunities for you to learn - and real learning is caught, not taught.

As you work through *Leaders' Journal* and seek to develop yourself you will need to:

- **See** your potential. Think big. Picture future success.

- **Choose** your way forward. Take decisions that lead to change. Don't just hope that you will drift in the right direction.

- **Do** new things and try them out. Stretch yourself every day. Take some risks; be prepared to fail.

- **Check** to see what progress is being made. Seek feedback and learn from both success and failure. Adapt your approaches.

- **Be** inspired and enthused by what you are learning. Share it with others. Let it change your way of thinking and how you see things.

As you discover something new through what you "do", it will affect the way you "see" things. Similarly as you "choose" a priority it could help you "be" more inspired and focused. Don't forget to check and reflect. Your learning and development will be dynamic and interconnected, not procedural.

Don't worry about it being perfect. Even Michelangelo's jottings didn't look great at first (I'm guessing!)

Wayne Gretzky, the former Canadian ice hockey player, said: "You miss 100 percent of the shots you never take."

Take some shots, but learn as you go.

P.S. We have included a "See, Choose, Do, Check, Be self-assessment" in The Really Useful Appendix on page 125. It will help you to focus your thinking and doing as you go through the rest of the Journal.

Descartes said: "To do is to be"...
Voltaire wrote: "To be is to do"...
Frank Sinatra sang: "Do be do be do"

4. Get the most from *Leaders' Journal*

Leaders' Journal is all about being and doing.

There are 40 days of readings and journal. We've organised it into an eight-week programme - five days of readings each week with two days to review the week.

The self-coaching process is simple: *read... reflect... explore... choose... write... do... review. The doers amongst us will tend to: read (possibly!)...choose...do. The thinkers will prefer to: read ...reflect (a lot!)...explore...write...review.* Over the next eight weeks may the doers think and the thinkers do!

Every day we will link you to **The Really Useful Appendix** (starting on page 121). It provides some great additional ideas, sources and tools for you to try and use.

As in the example on the facing page, the journal gives you the opportunity to jot down your thoughts each day in a few different ways:

Takeaways - your reflections, insights and anything you plan to try or change.

Pivotal moment - make a note of one potential pivotal moment that you are *anticipating* for the upcoming day. It could be a conversation you intend to have, a decision that you want to make, a meeting you have planned or an important task or mail.

The best way for you to get the highest return from the journal is to:

- allocate about ten minutes each day.
- don't do more than one day's reading in a day
- write something on the journal page every day
- at least check out the Really Useful Appendix each day, and work with those that work for you
- share what you learn with others

This is your Journal – it is your servant, not your master.

Example: DAY Z

"If at first you don't succeed then skydiving definitely isn't for you." Steve Wright

TAKEAWAY

I need to listen more and ask more questions. I should start with a question! ... rather than a statement.

Look at YouTube video.

PIVOTAL MOMENT

Meet Rajesh from ACME Media at 11.30. Get there early. Ask how his wife's pregnancy is going. Discuss the benefits of replacing Sergio with Zara as Global Account Manager...... I need his commitment and support.

The Really Useful Appendix Z
Look at three different ways to turn a statement into a great question.

Section B
40 Days

Week 1
You

"Play to your strengths."
"I haven't got any," said Harry, before he could stop himself.
"Excuse me," growled Moody, "you've got strengths if I say you've got them. Think now. What are you best at?"

From Harry Potter and the Goblet of Fire by J.K. Rowling,

Remember that people buy into the leader before they buy into the vision. Therefore we want to kick off the 40 days by getting you to think a bit more about yourself:

- How teachable are you?
- What do you really want?
- What can you be brilliant at?
- How do you see your role?
- How agile are you?

DAY 1

Leaders are teachable

GRAND SLAM

She was the first.

No Asian tennis player had ever won a Grand Slam singles tournament ... until Li Na.

And then, aged 31, Li Na appointed Carlos Rodriguez as her coach in place of her husband. Rodriguez helped her to the most successful years of her career as she became No. 2 in the world.

As Li Na became more successful, she had more coaching for fitness, diet and psychology as well as tennis. Yet in most people's work lives the more successful they become, the less time they give to develop themselves.

Paul Annacone, who coached Pete Sampras and Roger Federer, arguably the best tennis players ever, said of them both: "No matter how good you are as a player… you need a trusted pair of eyes because your own eyes can't see if everything is on course. Those players have immense skills, but one of their biggest strengths is often that they are incredibly stubborn and a good coach can go in and handle that mentality."

How teachable are you? How do you receive feedback?

If you are going to lead, you need to be learning and receiving – so stay a learner. How and from whom are you regularly learning and receiving?

Take a moment to answer those questions on the right-hand page. Identify a pivotal moment today when you can share this with a friend or colleague.

Invite them to ask you how it's going in a few days' time.

"It is the obligation of the ruler to continually renew himself in order to renew the people by his example."

Confucius

TAKEAWAY

PIVOTAL MOMENT

The Really Useful Appendix 1
All learning involves change. Use the GROW model to plan your personal change.

DAY 2

Your beliefs govern your choices

THE MANDELA CHALLENGE

I love films that make me think.

Justin Chadwick's *Mandela: Long Walk to Freedom* made me think. It chronicles Nelson Mandela's early life, coming of age, education and 27 years in prison before becoming President. When Mandela was questioned about the possibility of taking revenge on those who had committed atrocities, he replied: "I admit I want revenge, but I want something more than that... that is to live without fear and hatred."

His response "but I want something more" gives us an insight into one of the greatest leaders of his generation. He openly acknowledged his natural human feelings and responses to what had happened, but his overriding desire was for something better. It was his choice.

Your beliefs govern your choices. Your choices, not your situation, determine your character.

Your character as a leader will have a more telling impact upon your organisation, customers and people than your ability to manage the profit and loss, launch your latest product or even pull off a stellar acquisition. Whatever is at the top of an organisation filters down, as sure as water flows down the mountain.

What do you really want? What do you want to be the character of your organisation? Which of your personal characteristics do you want to promote or relegate?

How do you respond to the Mandela challenge? What is the "something more" that you want?

"Ever more people today have the means to live, but have no meaning to live for."

Victor E. Frankl

TAKEAWAY

PIVOTAL MOMENT

The Really Useful Appendix 2
See how what you believe affects your vocation and purpose.

DAY 3

Be brilliant at who you are!

BEST CARDS

You are the best at who you are - but a poor imitation of others.

At about the same time that Bill Gates was sneaking out of his student bedroom to use his university's computer, my brother was holed up in my school's computer room after school closed. He was a brilliant computer programmer, but not great at passing exams.

His school constantly gave him the message that he was a failure. But they failed – they failed to see or nurture his amazing talent and passion.

Fortunately, my brother didn't try to be someone else. He carried on developing software in his spare time and in the 1990s set up a very successful internet software business. He became the best in his field because he created the field. No-one else can do what he can do.

You can't be whatever you want to be - but you can be great at being you...

Success is born from identifying your strengths, developing them and utilising them.

You have unique strengths. You succeed when you play to your strengths. It is a case of "playing your best cards". Be crystal clear about what they are otherwise they will be difficult to play.

You will know in part what you excel at because you know what energises you - but you may have missed something. Be brave and objective and get some feedback from others. Ask a couple of friends or colleagues today for their view of when you are at your best.

Be brilliant at who you are!

"Nobody does it better…. Baby you're the best."
Carly Simon

TAKEAWAY

PIVOTAL MOMENT

The Really Useful Appendix 3
You can only "play the cards" you have … check out what
are your best cards.

DAY 4

Adopt the role of Chief Refresher

34.2% SALINITY

What's the lowest point on the earth's surface?

The Dead Sea.

It's 427 metres below sea level. The Dead Sea is a salt lake bordering Jordan and Israel. With 34.2% salinity it's 10 times saltier than the ocean and unsustainable for fish and animals, hence its unhealthy name.

Refreshing water flows in but because it's at the lowest point of the earth's surface nothing can flow out. There are timeless principles at work here. If things flow in, but they don't flow through and out, they are likely to die.

In your role as leader you can either be a "receiver" – the recipient of in-flow – or be a "refresher" – allowing what you receive to flow through and out. It is your choice, but only one of the models will sustain others. Let's focus on the Refresher model – how does it work?

First, let there be "flow-through". Let the insights that you glean about yourself, your business and your people percolate through. "Flow-through" occurs when you apply your new knowledge and let it work through your whole system.

Second, let there be "flow-out". There need to be outlets. Those you work with each day should be the direct recipients and practical beneficiaries of what you learn.

Irrespective of your personality and circumstance you have an opportunity right at the outset to determine to be either a "refresher" or just a "receiver".

Who are you investing in? Who are you encouraging, coaching and developing?

What would be the direct benefits to your relationships if you adopt the role of Chief Refresher?

Use the journal page to identify a pivotal moment today where you can refresh and renew someone.

"Great people are those who make others feel that they, too, can become great."

Mark Twain

TAKEAWAY

PIVOTAL MOMENT

The Really Useful Appendix 4
Look at your various roles as a leader in a fresh way, using the Greek Temple model.

DAY 5

Agility is a key leader behaviour

THE CHART TABLE

There was one rule on the ship - never put anything on the chart table, except the maps.

My friend, Ed, told me of when he was a young midshipman in the navy. It was early morning on the bridge. A small group of young officers were planning the day's voyage, when the visiting admiral popped his head around the door and called out, "Morning, chaps!"

"Would you like a mug of coffee, sir?"

The admiral was telling one of his wonderful stories when he received his coffee and put the mug on the table behind him - the chart table! The young officers didn't know what to say or do.

At that very moment the captain opened the door. He shouted, "Which of you ***!! sailors put the ***!! coffee mug on the ***!! chart table?"

A young officer broke the silence, "It was the admiral, sir."

The captain immediately retorted, "So then which of you ***!! sailors put the ***!! maps on the ***!! coffee table?"

Bursts of laughter broke the tension.

The captain's example may not be one you want to follow, but it is important for a leader to be agile. That means being prepared to adapt.

Agility is a key leader behaviour for the 21st century.

This doesn't mean saying or doing just whatever suits the situation, but it does mean taking on board new information and responding appropriately – even with humour. Recognise when you have got it wrong and put it right.

Is there a decision to make or a response to someone where you need to flex and make some adjustments today?

"The things we fear most in organizations—fluctuations, disturbances, imbalances—are the primary source of creativity."
Margaret J. Wheatley

TAKEAWAY

PIVOTAL MOMENT

The Really Useful Appendix 5
Daniel Goleman identified six leadership styles. Find out how many you can use.

Week 2
Your people

"Human beings the world over need freedom and security that they may be able to realise their full potential"

Aung San Suu Kyi

We turn the attention away from you and onto your team – your crew.

During Week 2 we are not aiming to tackle the A-Z of team leadership – we simply want to put it front and centre on your agenda. We will highlight some key principles to build an even more successful team and to help you decide what to keep at the top of your priority list. We will also suggest some practicalities for you to keep in mind.

As you go through this week think deeply about your team. Talk to them, listen to them, learn from them - and laugh together:

- What can you achieve together?
- What are your ambitions for them?
- What are their ambitions?
- What works well now?
- Where is the most important gap?
- What can you do differently?

DAY 6

Find the right people

LIVID

It still makes me livid even now when I think about it!

As a parent-governor on the School Board I was on the selection panel for the appointment of the new principal. There were two final candidates. The school had been well run, but now needed fresh direction and impetus. One candidate stood head and shoulders above the other, who was pleasant but ineffectual.

The old-fashioned interview and selection process came down to a vote. The chairperson announced that Mr Pleasant had beaten Ms Dynamic by 7 votes to 2. I couldn't believe it.

They had opted for the easy, no threat, option ... and they watched as the school went downhill for the next three years, but not before the principal went off sick with stress. Needless to say we moved our children to another school within months.

Having the right people on board is the single biggest issue for any enterprise today. Knowing what to do is not the biggest challenge - finding the person to do it is. So, find the right people.

If you hire the wrong person at the top of an organisation they can destroy it in no time at all. This applies to all key roles. Choose people you can trust. Competence usually improves, character generally doesn't. The right experience may qualify someone to get to the starting line, but their personality and attitude will enable them to win the race.

Choosing the right people becomes your top priority as a leader.

Look for winners, not starters.

"You don't train attitudes, you have to hire them."
Richard Branson

TAKEAWAY

PIVOTAL MOMENT

The Really Useful Appendix 6
Use the simple "hiring for success" framework when you
next recruit.

DAY 7

Use your people's talent – or lose it.

THE TWIST

Talent management is big business because it addresses how we make the most of human potential.

"Talent" means a natural aptitude or skill, but let's look at the origins of the word to understand more.

It became popularised by Jesus' parable of the talents. A parable was an everyday story with a meaning, usually with a twist. To set the scene a "talent" was a sum of money. Each talent was worth around $1m at today's value. Jesus' parable went something like this...

The CEO of a private equity business planned to be travelling for some time and didn't want his money just sitting there. He allocated $6m for investment and by his return it had nearly doubled. An impressive result, but he wasn't fully happy. Why?

The entrepreneur had three managers with different abilities. They were allocated the monies according to their ability. The top manager doubled his $3m to $6m. Number two also doubled his money from $2m to $4m. Both were promoted.

Number three, however, was seriously risk averse. He just sat on the money and simply returned his allocation of $1m. He was promptly fired. Ouch... the guy who had least lost everything. That was the twist.

You may think the moral of the story is, "Make the most of what you've got", but you could see it slightly differently - "If you don't use it, you lose it".

Be clear: use your people's talent or lose it. Don't let their potential slip through your fingers.

What could be a pivotal moment for you today?

"In most cases being a good boss means hiring talented people and then getting out of their way."

Tina Fey

TAKEAWAY

PIVOTAL MOMENT

The Really Useful Appendix 7
Find nine simple but powerful questions to help develop
and challenge your team members.

DAY 8

Appreciate your people

VALENTINES

I felt a bit embarrassed as I crept into my Atlanta office late one evening to put flowers on everyone's desk.

I'd just heard a very motivational talk about the "power of appreciation". With Valentine's Day fast approaching I decided to show some simple appreciation for everyone in my team and bought everyone some flowers and a gift card.

The speaker had emphasised the importance of the personal touch, so I decided to hand-write some letters. It wasn't difficult to come up with the qualities and examples that I liked and appreciated about everyone, even the team members that I found challenging. It took some time, but I really enjoyed doing something so positive and focusing on their good qualities and celebrating our successes.

Every team member came up to me and thanked me. Many sent handwritten notes back. A few years later, even after I had moved back to London, I noted that more than one of the team still had the handwritten letter pinned up above their desk.

This wasn't a natural action for me. I realised that my focus on poor performance had often translated into insecurity and a lack of trust in my team. Positive, genuine appreciation, at unexpected moments, will be very motivating.

Jennifer Chatman, of the University of California, conducted experiments in which she tried to find a point at which flattery became ineffective. It turned out there wasn't one!

Expressing appreciation, however, is much more than flattery and occasional gifts. Simple and genuine "pleases" and "thank yous" are normal courtesies that can easily be overlooked in challenging work environments.

So who are you going to thank today?

"Praise works with only three types of people – men, women and children."

Anon

TAKEAWAY

PIVOTAL MOMENT

The Really Useful Appendix 8
Use Gallup's research to measure your team's engagement.

DAY 9

Build your people's confidence

ITALIAN BAKED PIE

What is the volume of an Italian baked pie?

The pie consists of a round base of dough topped with tomatoes and cheese. It has a radius of "z" and height "a"?

The answer is Pi × z × z × a.

So what's the connection between mathematics and leadership?

You need to think mathematically about your people.

You can divide your people, add to them, take away from them or multiply them. I am not talking about increasing or decreasing the numbers in your organisation, but about increasing or decreasing the very individuals who work with you.

I have seen executives humiliate individuals and destroy their confidence and trust. I have also seen passive leadership imperceptibly erode people's motivation. Fortunately, I've also witnessed many examples where a true leader has genuinely added and helped grow their people and even multiply their self-belief and performance.

Confidence is a fragile commodity, but key to success. Have you ever seen a sports star lose their confidence? A brilliant player can become a weak performer overnight. It's no different in your team.

Confidence is a complex topic. It can be confidence to do a task well, social confidence or a sense of self-worth - and they are often interrelated. There is no "confidence tablet" that you can prescribe, but demonstrating that you believe in your people will go a long way. This will require different strokes for different folks.

Find ways to build your people's confidence and watch them thrive.

How can you **+** or **x** the confidence of one of your team today?

"I feel really grateful to the people who encouraged me and helped me develop. Nobody can succeed on their own."

Sheryl Sandberg

TAKEAWAY

PIVOTAL MOMENT

The Really Useful Appendix 9
Assess the confidence of those you lead and think of ways you could boost it.

DAY 10

Do the vision

TERRIBLE NEWS

"I am leaving."

I was 18 months into my new job and the star in my team told me she was joining a direct competitor. I was distraught. This was terrible news for the business and a big blow for me personally. In my first significant leadership role, I had failed to retain the strongest member of the team.

So why did she leave?

She explained that when I had arrived, I shared an exciting vision about a growing business expanding into new areas of work. This convinced her to stay on. However, I had listened to the concerns of the team about previous eras of "boom and bust" and stuck to our traditional core business and hired no-one.

There is a simple principle about learning. It's called "70-20-10". 70% of learning takes place on the job, 20% through mentoring and 10% in the classroom. By not expanding her into new areas of work, I'd not delivered on 70% of her learning.

I started to invest time in new products and hiring. It wasn't popular with some of the team, who made a lot of noise. However, the business grew and became an exciting place to work, full of opportunity. We hired and retained some great people. Unnervingly, some were better than me!

The big lesson for me was that there can't be a disconnect between what you say you'll do and what you do. The vision must be evidenced by what we do.

It wasn't that my team saw me hiring again that was important, but that I had started to "do the vision" again – doing what I said we would do. This engenders trust and commitment.

How are you doing that?

Never, for the sake of peace and quiet, deny your own experience and convictions."

Dag Hammarskjold

TAKEAWAY

PIVOTAL MOMENT

The Really Useful Appendix 10

Building trust is fundamental to building successful teams. Check out Patrick Lencioni's model on team effectiveness.

Week 3
See the big picture

"Leaders are fascinated by the future ... As a leader, you are never satisfied with the present, because in your head you can see a better future ..."

Steve Jobs

This week give yourself some more time and space to be fascinated by the future, because that is where we are all heading.

Over the next five days we hope that you will be challenged not just to think ahead, but also to see more things around you - and see them in a different light. The greatest sportspeople play with their "head up". They see the whole game. They have vision. They seem to have more time and space than anybody else. They spot the opportunity to attack and also know when to defend. They see the right play at the right time.

Keep your head up, create space and time ... and enjoy the game!

DAY 11

Keep your eyes wide open

THE STUMBLING MAN

I am an avid ball sports fan and for many years I played rugby.

Late one winter Saturday afternoon I travelled home after a game. I parked in Greenwich Park to take in the fantastic panorama over London and listen to the sports results.

It was dark, the radio and heater were both on, the lights over London were magnificent and I was cosy. The next thing I knew somebody was tapping loudly on the car window and shining a torch in.

It was a policeman.

I had been fast asleep. I had no idea what was happening as I stumbled out of the car.

The policeman explained that the park gates had been locked. He queried my stumbling out of the car and asked whether I had been drinking. He insisted that I take a breath test. When it was totally clear, he insisted I repeat it. He couldn't believe this stumbling man was sober.

I had some explaining to do when I got home. Rather than "seeing the big picture" of London, I had been breathalysed in a parked car in a locked park.

The moral of the story is: keep your eyes wide open!

Why not practise looking at different things or looking at things differently?

Why not take a different route to work? When you arrive linger a while and look at the outside of your building. Look at the reception area. What do they say about your organisation? Observe the movement of people. Take a different seat in meetings. Look and listen more.

Discuss fresh observations about your business with your team.

"Perspective is everything when you are experiencing the challenges of life."

Joni Eareckson Tada

TAKEAWAY

PIVOTAL MOMENT

The Really Useful Appendix 11
Find out whether your team are on the same page as you or seeing things differently.

DAY 12

See the connections you need to make

A TO B

I love a unique name.

Isambard Kingdom Brunel. You don't hear many children with those names nowadays.

Isambard was the king of Victorian engineers. He was a visionary and had daring. He had big, grand ideas. He has gone down in history for making connections from A to B in as many different ways as possible - railways, tunnels, bridges and ships.

During his relatively short career he achieved many world firsts. Brunel assisted in the building of the first ever under-river tunnel and the first propeller-driven iron ship, the SS Great Britain, the largest ship ever built until the 20th century. He designed the Clifton Suspension Bridge, which went further and higher than any other bridge. His designs revolutionised public transport and modern engineering. He achieved great things.

Yes there were some spectacular failures, but Isambard Kingdom Brunel got results.

Reflecting on Brunel's unparalleled career, Professor Ross Peters argues that Brunel's genius, however, lay in his ability to get his ideas across to others. Without his ability to convince financiers and persuade stakeholders as well as inspire his workers, he would have accomplished little. Brunel knew he wanted to get from A to B, but he also needed to make great connections beyond his technical world. That also requires vision and daring.

We can easily get caught up in our own world. To make things happen you need to know who is in your "solar system". See the connections you need to make.

Who do you need to engage with to make it happen?

How can you engage with them?

"You can have brilliant ideas, but if you can't get them across, they won't get you anywhere."

Lee Iacocca

TAKEAWAY

PIVOTAL MOMENT

The Really Useful Appendix 12
Work out who are the most important people in your "solar system".

DAY 13

Think outside-in

CMRM

His store held the world record for the highest sales per square foot of any retail outlet.

Julian Richer opened his first electrical retail shop in London Bridge aged 19.

His company, Richer Sounds, competes very successfully in one of the lowest margin industries by providing expert advice. The stores are closed until midday every weekday so that the sales staff can learn the features of the latest flat screen TV, wireless streaming speaker or home cinema system.

Despite serving 12,000 customers a week, Richer responds personally to every customer complaint and gets an average of just two.

Richer Sounds now has over 50 stores across the UK and they all have the same passion for customer service.

Your business model will be very different from Richer Sounds, but how do you put the customer at the heart of your business?

How do you look to your customers?

I wish I could invent a CMRM – a Customer Mind-Reading Machine. The closest thing to it that is available on the market at present is some good, open questions, a pair of ears and a couple of legs to take you to your customer.

A critical part of seeing the big picture is to see it through your customer's eyes. Think outside-in.

You'll learn more in a day talking to customers than in a week of brainstorming or a month of market research. What could be your pivotal moment today?

"The magic formula that successful businesses have discovered is to treat customers like guests and employees like people."

Tom Peters

TAKEAWAY

PIVOTAL MOMENT

The Really Useful Appendix 13
Check to see if you are really a trusted adviser to your customers and clients.

DAY 14

Look inside the box

GORILLAS

It was a day I learnt I was not as observant as I thought.

We were shown a 30-second film of two teams playing basketball and told to count the number of passes made by the team in white.

The film started. I was in the zone and I got it. Yes, they made 15 passes!

But, in fact, I completely missed a key moment.

Just a few seconds into the film, someone dressed as a gorilla had slowly walked right into the middle of the basketball game. They stopped, beat their chest at the camera, and then casually sauntered off. Remarkably, almost everybody else watching the film missed the gorilla, just like me. My natural competitiveness meant that I was over-focused on counting the number of passes and didn't see what was happening right in front of me.

It's too easy to miss things that are going on right under our noses … opportunities or risks. In this instance an aggressive gorilla could have caused mayhem or maybe this gentle giant could have been the best marketing attraction ever.

Yes, as leader you need to see the big picture of what is happening in the outside world. You also need to have clear sight of what is happening on the inside world – within your organisation. It is valuable to think outside the box, but it is essential to see inside the box.

To see things differently you have to take a step back. Observe what is really happening in your organisation.

What is the gorilla in your room?

"I'll be more enthusiastic about encouraging thinking outside the box when there's evidence of any thinking going on inside it."

Terry Pratchett

TAKEAWAY

PIVOTAL MOMENT

The Really Useful Appendix 14
Have you spotted the gorilla in your situation? Get your team working together and use the Co-consulting method to look at your situation in a new way.

DAY 15

See the here and now

TIPPERARY

The driver wound down his window and asked the farmer, "How do I get to Tipperary?"

The farmer offered the unhelpful advice, "If you want to get there, I wouldn't start from here!"

I spend a lot of my time helping organisations and people on their journey to "get there from here". Often the problems of the "here and now" seem so overwhelming that there is no energy, time or space to even think of getting "there".

The optimist will dream about how great "there" will be. The pessimist does not like the sound of "there" or ever imagine getting away from "here". The realist will hold both the "here" and "there" equally in balance and work out what they need to do next.

In my experience the stronger the "here and now" is, the stronger the "there and future" will be. That is true both at an individual and organisational level.

Leaders are by nature future-oriented. Seeing the bigger picture may appear to be just about what lies ahead, but it is not. Be mindful of the "here and now" - it provides the best platform for your future success. It helps you to be grounded and practical. It prevents you from merely fantasising about your ideal future and enables you to address the upcoming challenges.

See and make the most of "the here and now"

What do you value about your current position and circumstances? Have you expressed this to the people around you?

"He who is not contented with what he has, would not be contented with what he would like to have."

Socrates

TAKEAWAY

PIVOTAL MOMENT

The Really Useful Appendix 15
Take the Big Health Check and review the challenges of your "here and now".

Week 4

Choose the right direction

"The essence of strategy is choosing what not to do"
Michael Porter

Leadership involves making choices. As I was told when I was younger, "You can't have your cake and eat it."

You have to weigh things up and then decide.

"Decide" is a killer word. Suicide, fratricide, pesticide, homicide are all "killer words" - to kill yourself, a brother, an insect or another person. To "decide", therefore means to kill off or cut off all the alternatives.

Having worked across hundreds of organisations I have found that the most successful know which routes to take and which alternatives to kill off.

Over the next five days you will be thinking about your direction and the alternatives facing you. This week's insights and exercises should help you choose which routes to take and which to kill off.

DAY 16

Understand the Why

DEBT-FREE

"This is the wrong direction!"

It was early morning. I'd just changed jobs and was driving to my new office. I was lost in thought about the day ahead. Then, after 20 minutes, it dawned on me ... I'm heading back to my old place of work. Madness.

I was driving on auto-pilot. I'd got in the car and the car was taking me to where it had been going for the last five years. I wasn't driving ...the car was!

It's easy to live life on auto-pilot – going through the motions, with the appearance of control, but not knowing where you're heading or why you're doing what you're doing.

Some years ago I was speaking with a colleague. She was a mum with two small children who put long hours into her work. I asked what she wanted from life.

"To be debt-free".

I asked why she wanted this. She answered and then I asked "why?" again. She finally said "I want to create happy family memories".

Then it dawned on us. Choosing long hours made sense to be debt–free, but perhaps creating happy family memories meant choosing to work *less* hours.

If we can't articulate where we're going and why, we're in danger of making poor choices. We've no basis to navigate. Everything becomes a priority.

I was in "drive-mode"; my colleague was in "do-mode". Only after we addressed the *where* and *why* questions were we able to zig and zag back into the right direction.

You are the leader. So where are you going and why?

"Every single person ... knows what they do... some know how they do it ... but very, very few people know why they do what they do"

Simon Sinek

TAKEAWAY

PIVOTAL MOMENT

The Really Useful Appendix 16
You know what you do and probably how you do it - but do you know why?

DAY 17

Prioritise your priorities

TOO BROKE TO MANAGE

Do you have any broken windows?

In 1982, social scientists James Q. Wilson and George L. Kelling introduced what they called the "broken windows" theory. They observed that in neighbourhoods where one broken window was left unrepaired, the remaining windows would soon be broken, too. Eventually this could lead to more serious crime.

During his second term as New York's Mayor, Rudy Giuliani was determined to put the broken windows theory into action. Despite New York's infamous image of being "too big, too unruly, too diverse, too broke to manage", he wanted to prove the city was, in fact, manageable. This led to a dramatic reduction in crime in New York when efforts were made to stamp out minor offences such as graffiti and accosting people for money on the street.

The same principle applies inside organisations.

This is most evident when it comes to the values you claim to hold. Tolerating abuse of your organisation's values particularly by top performers or senior people is a perfect way to lose your direction and the commitment of your people. Giuliani did not go without his critics with his "zero tolerance" policy and neither will you.

Of course you choose the priorities and you choose to live by them. If you say that customer service is your highest priority, but don't address rude or poor customer service, people won't believe you.

Prioritise your priorities.

Where are your broken windows? What is going to be pivotal for you today?

"The main thing is to make the main thing the main thing."
Stephen Covey

PIVOTAL MOMENT

TAKEAWAY

The Really Useful Appendix 17
Priorities are about what is most important. Sort out the important from the urgent using the Eisenhower Matrix.

DAY 18

Choose your golden rules

CHICAGO

Easy Eddie was probably the top earning lawyer in Chicago in the 1920s. He worked for Al Capone, the legendary Mafia boss.

One day, he determined it was more important for him to pass on a good name, rather than money, to his son. He decided to turn state evidence against Capone and he testified about his tax avoidance. Capone was sent to the notorious Alcatraz jail. Easy Eddie knew it would cost him his life. On November 8th 1939 he was gunned down in his car.

Butch O'Hare was a top pilot in World War Two.

On February 20th 1942 the aircraft carrier USS Lexington was attacked by nine Japanese bombers. Butch O'Hare single-handedly shot down three planes and chased the others away. He was the first US pilot in WW2 to be awarded the US Medal of Honor. Some years later Chicago's airport was named after him.

Butch O'Hare was Easy Eddie's son.

Our jobs, family and friends will always impact on each other. Easy Eddie eventually chose to live by a value which cost him his life. He left a legacy of bravery, which endured in his son.

What values are you known for in your day job? What values will you hold to your detriment? What adjectives might others use to describe you?

How are those values practically demonstrated in the decisions you make and the actions you take?

The lesson from the story of Easy Eddie O'Hare is that we choose our values, and upholding values is not always easy. Are there any choices that you want to make?

"Those are my principles, and if you don't like them … well, I have others."

Groucho Marx

TAKEAWAY

PIVOTAL MOMENT

The Really Useful Appendix 18
"Peel back the onion" to work out what your values are.

DAY 19

Set the right expectations

ICELANDIC WAITERS

In Iceland, waiters consider it an insult to be tipped. In most other places, it's expected.

Expectations drive behaviours.

As a proficient squash player, I was challenged to a game by a new co-worker. He wasn't the slimmest player in the world. I thought it was going to be a walkover.

It was – I lost five games to one!

I came far below my own expectations, but well above his – he was surprised I even won a game! Next time I changed my expectations.

Success is measured against expectations. If we do better than expected we feel delighted; if we do worse we feel miserable. Feelings and perceptions are important. Just consider the phenomenon of stock prices rising even when a company announces bad news, simply because the news wasn't as bad as expected.

Understanding, setting and managing expectations is a critical dimension of your leadership role. It may be the expectations of the market, your customer, your team, your family or yourself. It's very easy not to meet expectations.

How do you get it right?

Well, much of the time it's within your gift to set the right expectations. Of course there will be competing expectations, but remember you can't please everybody. If you try, you'll be run ragged.

Make it a conscious choice. Be crystal clear, so that everybody else is clear. And keep checking to see if expectations have changed. That's your job.

Could you realign some expectations today to ensure others are following the right direction? It may even be a pivotal moment.

"The first step in exceeding your customer's expectations is to know those expectations."

Roy H. Williams

TAKEAWAY

PIVOTAL MOMENT

The Really Useful Appendix 19
You might have some great answers, but are you asking the right questions? Find some tips and tricks for asking great questions.

DAY 20

Choose your choices

WHAT'S YOUR DING?

Steve Jobs said his ambition was to "put a ding in the Universe".

He did just that.

But when he was at college, he dropped out to *drop in*. He dropped out of his scheduled classes to drop in on classes which he had no right to be at. In this unexpected way he became fascinated by, of all things, calligraphy. He later credited this passion and skill as the inspiration for the ground-breaking design at Apple.

What motivated him?

He was acutely aware, long before his battle with cancer, that one day he would die. So he asked himself: "If today were the last day of my life, would I want to do what I am about to do today?" And if he said "No" too many times, he chose to change something. He credited this philosophy with helping him make the big choices in his life.

Whatever you are doing now is the result of choices you have made – whether they were conscious or unconscious. We all face pressures that constrain us, some more than others. Ultimately how we respond to those pressures is, equally, our choice.

Steve Jobs urged people not to live other people's lives, but choose their own. Don't waste your life living other people's lives, not even Steve Jobs'.

What is your ding? What choices will you make to make it happen?

If this were to be the last day of your life, would you want to do what you are about to do? It's your choice.

"He is no fool who gives what he cannot keep to gain what he cannot lose."

Jim Elliot

TAKEAWAY

PIVOTAL MOMENT

The Really Useful Appendix 20
Start planning for the day you die.

Week 5

Do the right things

"Management is doing things right; leadership is doing the right things."

Peter Drucker

What separates successful from unsuccessful enterprises?

They do the right things ... and they do them first. They put first things first. How do you work out what are the right things? In *Leaders' Map* we introduced a new way to classify everything you decide and do. The five classifications are:

Transformative – decisions that could be **G**ame-changers

Creative – things that "turn on the **L**ight"

Proactive –actions that are **E**nterprising

Productive – **P**roducing things efficiently

Reactive –responding to events which you may want to **S**top

We called the classification system **"GLEPS™"**. Every action, conversation, decision, event or communication fits into one of these five classifications or GLEPS. You may choose how you classify or GLEP a particular action. For example I buy flowers for my wife - it could be:

- reactive (in response to "you never buy flowers for me.")

- productive (to make the house look more welcoming for visitors)

- proactive (to remind her that it's our anniversary – she always forgets!)

- creative (she's done a flower arranging course and I've learnt something)

- transformative (who knows where this might lead?)

How I GLEP it will influence the way I approach it ... and also her response!

If you view a decision as transformative, treat it as a potential game-changer. You may see that a conversation could be creative and then give it enough time. If the task, however, is purely productive, work out how to handle it efficiently. If you want take the initiative at an event you will need to be proactive. Alternatively, when you consider a meeting to be reactive, then you may want to save time and stop it.

Each day this week we'll consider a different GLEP. So, start to assign a GLEP to each of your key decisions and actions and let it change the way you think about and approach them.

Start GLEPPING!

DAY 21

Look to be transformative

THE SCRAPBOOK

In December 1938 London stockbroker Nicholas Winton was planning his skiing holiday in Switzerland.

He decided, however, to visit his friend Martin Blake in Prague first. He saw first-hand the plight of Jewish families facing Nazi persecution. Instead of going skiing he ended up helping them.

Winton found homes in Britain for 669 children, many of whose parents perished in Auschwitz. Eight trains reached London. The ninth did not. It was due to leave on September 1, carrying 250 children — the largest number yet. That day Germany invaded Poland, and all borders were closed.

After the war he kept quiet about his exploits. The truth came out in 1988 when his wife Grete found a scrapbook in their attic. It contained lists of children's names. He then explained what he had done 50 years previously.

An estimated 6,000 people across the world are descendants of 'Nicky's Children'.

He was knighted by the Queen in 2003.

His daughter, Barbara, said "What he did in 1939 wasn't out of character. It was typical of the kind of impulses he has when he sees a situation and thinks it should be rectified."

Nicholas Winton was a game-changer. He didn't have plans to change 669, and ultimately 6,000, people's lives; he was just prepared to act. He just did the right thing on one day. It wasn't out of character. The transformative outcomes just followed.

Look to be transformative. Explore ways in which you can be a game-changer in your situation.

Watch the moment Nicholas Winton met some of the survivors he saved on YouTube: https://www.youtube.com/watch?v=6_nFuJAF5F0

"Boldness has genius, power and magic in it."
Goethe

TAKEAWAY

PIVOTAL MOMENT

The Really Useful Appendix 21
Find more about GLEPS on page 146 and check how you can
be more transformative.

DAY 22

Let your creative juices flow

A HUNDRED PARAKEETS

Bill Thomas saw despair in every room.

As a young physician, in upstate New York, Bill Thomas took on his new job as medical director. His business was the care of 80 elderly residents who were physically disabled and/or had Alzheimer's disease.

The nursing home depressed him. So he tried to fix it the only way he knew. He did examinations and scans and changed medications. Little changed, except that the medical costs were driven up.

Then he looked at things differently. He diagnosed three plagues: boredom, loneliness and helplessness. His solution was to put life back into the home.

That's what he did – literally. He put green plants in every room, organised a vegetable and flower garden and brought in two dogs, four cats and a hundred parakeets - all contrary to the New York nursing home regulations. The fact that the parakeets arrived before their cages only added to the complete pandemonium.

Researchers found that prescriptions halved, total drug costs reduced to 38% of comparative facilities and death rates fell by 15%. Bill Thomas had looked at the situation differently from others. In the bleakest circumstance he saw the opportunity for life and then creative ideas started to flow.

Why not discover your inner Leonardo and get your team together to discuss new ways of "turning on the light"?

Think about your customers and your people. Be inquisitive. In what way would you like them to feel differently? What would delight them?

Let your creative juices flow. Suspend early judgement on the ideas people generate – let them breathe and develop them.

"We don't grow into creativity, we grow out of it. Or rather, we get educated out of it."

Sir Ken Robinson

TAKEAWAY

PIVOTAL MOMENT

The Really Useful Appendix 22
When have you been most creative in the past? Work out some ways to be creative in the future.

DAY 23

Being proactive means being first

USAIN BOLT

"I'm going to be first. I'm going to win."

He said it nonchalantly, without bravado or arrogance. Josh, my son, was five years old at the time, and was just sharing the fact of what would happen.

It was his first race ever - the sports day sprint. He wasn't normally given to making such bold proclamations nor was he a budding Usain Bolt. To avoid unnecessary disappointment, Jackie, my wife, said, "I'm sure you'll enjoy it and do your best. That is what is important."

Without any surprise after he came first, he simply commented, "I said I would."

Being first. What a great position to be. If only we could just say it and it would come to pass.

Well, the good news is – you can! At least most of the time you can, if you really want to.

You can be the first to set up the meeting, the first to smile, the first to shake hands, the first to say thank you, the first to say "congratulations", the first to listen, the first to say "I don't understand", the first to ask a wise question, the first to challenge a wrong direction, the first to say "how can I help you?"

You can choose what you want to be first at - and then just do it.

Being proactive, being enterprising, is all about choosing to be first and then doing it. That is why it is called "taking the 1nitiative"!

What do you want to be first at today? Why not make a note on the journal page about how you are going to reach out?

"Opportunities multiply as they are seized."
Sun Tzu

TAKEAWAY

PIVOTAL MOMENT

The Really Useful Appendix 23
Find some examples of how you can be proactive and
decide what you want to be "first" in.

DAY 24

Be productive - work smart and hard

683,806 HOURS

I recently asked a senior executive, "What do you want?"

His immediate response - "More time!" - will be echoed by many, probably including you and me.

Every day we spend 24 hours of our average 683,806 lifetime quota. The productivity and time management industry is booming: "How can we do more in less time?"

Many centuries ago another senior executive was asked, "What do you want?" King Solomon replied, "Wisdom".

For all our frenetic efforts to stop the grains from descending in the egg-timer, perhaps we need to apply ourselves more to wisdom. Wisdom can give us perspective.

Solomon gave his perspective on time-management and productivity when he wrote:

"There is a time for everything and a season for every activity under the heavens: a time to be born and a time to die … a time to plant and a time to uproot … a time to mourn and a time to dance … a time to search and a time to give up … a time to be silent and a time to speak … a time for war and a time for peace."

Many of us live in "urban time" and have lost a proper sense of the seasons – the natural time to do things. Wisdom is the discernment to work out the right time and season for everything. Timing is key to success – *when* do you need to do something? Then just do it!

Be productive - work smart and hard at doing the right things at the right time.

What is wisdom telling you about being productive today?

"Time is the scarcest resource and unless it is managed nothing else can be managed."

Peter Drucker

TAKEAWAY

PIVOTAL MOMENT

The Really Useful Appendix 24
Chart the key productive activities that you need to tackle in the coming week.

DAY 25

Be prepared to say 'No'

JUST 15 MINUTES

"All you have to do is wait."

The researcher was talking to a group of four- to six-year-olds. The children had been allowed to select a single treat. They were then told that if they waited for just 15 minutes before eating the treat, they would then be given a second treat.

Some waited and some didn't.

The research was being conducted in a US kindergarten in the 1960s. Follow-up studies over the years showed that there was a strong correlation between the ability to delay gratification in that nursery and various forms of "life success" later in life, in terms of education and employment.

Not surprising, you say. But you and I face the same test nearly every waking minute of every day.

We live in an age of massive information overload. In 1976 there were 9,000 products in the average supermarket; today there are 40,000. And yet most of our shopping is covered by 150 items. The noise screaming for our attention is not reducing, but is also becoming more immediate.

How many times a day do you check your mobile devices just in case somebody wants your attention?

There is a need to be "master and not slave" to the information flow. Our success is also linked to our ability to delay gratification or just say "No."

The most successful leaders are "self-leaders". To stop being reactive be prepared to say "No".

What do you need to delay or say "No" to today?

"Never forget that only dead fish swim with the stream."
Malcolm Muggeridge

PIVOTAL MOMENT

TAKEAWAY

The Really Useful Appendix 25
Write down your own "stopping list".

Week 6
Check progress

"We all want progress, but if you're on the wrong road, progress means doing an about-turn and walking back to the right road; in that case, the man who turns back soonest is the most progressive."

C.S. Lewis

C.S. Lewis hits the nail on the head. The most important question is whether you are heading in the right direction. Don't lose sight of that question this week as you look at the progress you are making.

There is nothing better than to know that you are heading in the right direction, with the sun shining and the wind behind you. Celebrate the moment!

Checking progress also means asking: "Have we done what we said we would do and achieved what we said we would achieve?"

If things need to be fixed, don't just "kick the tyres" and hope for the best. Leadership is not about having another good idea, but achieving results - through others. Follow-through is often the determining factor as to whether you succeed or just miss out.

But don't just look back, look forward. Check the weather conditions again. Demonstrate your agility to tack and turn at the right moment. Hold your nerve and take your people with you.

DAY 26

Seek honest feedback

THE MERCHANT OF DEATH

How did the name of the man who invented dynamite become synonymous with peace?

He had some very unusual feedback and he decided to do something about it.

Albert B. Nobel (1833 -1896) amassed a fortune by producing explosives. Nowadays this Swedish munitions manufacturer is best known for the Nobel prizes for literature, economics, sciences - and peace. The Nobel Peace Prize has been awarded to a range of luminaries – Barack Obama, Aung Sang Suu Kyi, Nelson Mandela, the 14th Dalai Lama, Desmond Tutu, Mother Teresa ... and in 2014 to the youngest ever winner, 17-year-old Malala Yousafzai.

When Nobel's brother died, a French newspaper mistook the death of his brother Ludvig for his, headlining his obituary *"The merchant of death is dead."*

"Dr Alfred Nobel, who made his fortune by finding a way to kill the most people as ever before in the shortest time possible, died yesterday," the newspaper wrote.

What he read horrified him. He became obsessed by his potential legacy and changed his will to establish the prestigious prizes for peace and progress.

It is a short case study of the power of honest, objective and timely feedback.

If you are to check progress you will need people around you who will be prepared to be brutally honest. Seek honest feedback and don't stop seeking it. Be prepared to listen to your partner when they say "You can't be serious!", or a friend who raises the question, "Are you sure?"

Who will give you the best view as to whether you are on track?

> *"You drown not by falling into a river, but by staying submerged in it."*
> Paulo Coelho

TAKEAWAY

PIVOTAL MOMENT

The Really Useful Appendix 26
Effective listening is the key to benefitting from feedback.
Discover five tips to improve your skills.

DAY 27

Face up to reality

THE ELEPHANT

In 1864, in Spotsylvania County, Virginia, another battle in the American Civil War was raging.

Major General John Sedgwick, a Union officer, scolded his men for taking cover from enemy fire. To prove his point he stood up and spoke what were to be his very last words:

"They couldn't even hit an elephant at this distance."

Seconds later the sniper's bullet got him just below his left eye.

Yes, leaders may inspire their followers to great ambitions and acts of courage, but a lack of honest realism can ruin businesses, derail careers … and even cost lives.

Jim Collins, in his book *Good to Great,* speaks about the need to face the brutal facts of your current reality. Collins sees the honesty to see and say things as they really are as a core attribute of the most effective leaders.

Winston Churchill, a more successful wartime leader than Sedgwick, said "Facts are better than dreams."

On taking over as the British Prime Minister on 10 May 1940, eight months after the start of World War Two in the most perilous of circumstances, Churchill's assessment was "I have nothing to offer but blood, toil, tears and sweat." This formed the platform for an arduous defence, a slow change of fortune and eventual victory.

When the going gets tough, say it as it is. Face up to reality. Be honest with both the figures and your people.

What "facts" do you need to check again to ensure you make the progress you want?

"It is better to lead from behind and to put others in front; especially when you celebrate victory ... You take the front line when there is danger. Then people will appreciate your leadership."

Nelson Mandela

TAKEAWAY

PIVOTAL MOMENT

The Really Useful Appendix 27
Face the facts. Check your progress against your journey plan.

DAY 28

Adapt or die

EASY LUNCH

The dodo was "born to fly".

The three foot tall, 50-pound dodo bird was first glimpsed by Dutch settlers who landed on Mauritius in 1598. Seventy-five years later, the dodo was extinct.

At some stage flying became too hard work and waddling took over. They probably read about the extinction of the ancient Archaeopteryx in their history lessons and said, "It will never happen to us." But it did.

Why did the dodo vanish so quickly?

Mauritius had changed radically and the dodo did not "check progress." Gone were the easy times when the birds could wander freely. They became "easy lunch" for Dutch sailors and were then finished off by their domesticated animals.

The message is clear. Adapt to the world as it is, not as it was.

Economies must adapt to the dynamic changes of globalisation and technology. Businesses should flex to the changing needs of customers. Even hiring new people requires conscious adjustments. That means doing things differently or doing different things and doing them quickly enough.

Don't let things drift. Adapt or die. Complacency is the greatest enemy of change.

Once Chief Dodo started to see the numbers of Dutch settlers increase and the numbers of his dodo compadres decrease he should have done something … quickly!

Diagnose your situation. If your business was a human body, how fit would you say it is? What would the health check say? If you were the company doctor what would you be advising your patient?

Don't delay.

"Procrastinate now. Don't put it off!"
Ellen DeGeneres

TAKEAWAY

PIVOTAL MOMENT

The Really Useful Appendix 28
What stage is your team at, and what do they need from
you as their leader?

DAY 29

Appreciate your assets

THE SANTA MONICA WAREHOUSE

William Randolph Hearst was the most powerful newspaper publisher of the 1920s.

He invested a huge fortune in collecting works of art for his fabled Californian home, Hearst Castle. He collected antiques and *objets d'art* from around the world and stored them in warehouses.

One day he came across the description of a rare piece of art in *Creative Arts* magazine. It was to become his next target and so he commissioned a number of agents to track it down. Months went by. Finally his own agent returned empty-handed from the global search, but reported to Hearst that the item had at last been found.

Hearst asks "Where was it found?"

The agent replied, "It was in your Santa Monica warehouse. You bought it years ago."

When you check progress and do a stock-check of your assets it's important to value and celebrate what you already have. Appreciate your assets. Not only is it good for you, but it's mightily important for those who are working with you.

Be careful of the "new toy syndrome". Sometimes when we think we are missing out on something, the solution is to be found inside the organisation. Make sure that you haven't overlooked or undervalued some asset that you already have.

As you navigate towards your next opportunity or around a tricky obstacle why not check that you haven't overlooked somebody who could really help you? Look a bit deeper and a bit wider.

Which "assets" have you under-appreciated? What could be a pivotal moment today?

"A thankful heart is not only the greatest of virtues, but the parent of all other virtues."

Cicero

TAKEAWAY

PIVOTAL MOMENT

The Really Useful Appendix 29
Check out Belbin's Team Roles to see how to appreciate the capabilities or different roles of your colleagues.

DAY 30

Communicate the change

THE PAPERWEIGHT

John F Kennedy probably thought his war was over on 2nd August 1943.

He was a commander of a torpedo boat during World War Two when his vessel was rammed by a Japanese destroyer in the Solomon Sea. The boat was halved by the impact and two sailors died, but Kennedy and ten of his men swam to the island of Nauru. Communication lines were completely cut off and JFK and his fellow survivors had only coconuts and fresh water to keep them alive.

Six days later two Solomon Islanders, Biuku Gasa and Eroni Kumana, turned up in their dugout canoe.

The two groups couldn't communicate in the same language, so Biuku Gasa gestured that Kennedy send a message on a coconut shell. He inscribed:

"Nauru Isl commander / native knows position / he can pilot / 11 alive / need small boat / Kennedy."

The two Solomon Islanders took the coconut and rowed their dugout canoe at great risk through 65 km of hostile waters to the Allied base at Rendova, enabling a successful rescue operation. Later Kennedy had the shell made into a paperweight which he kept in the Oval Office.

Kennedy understood first-hand that you can be shipwrecked unexpectedly. The situation had radically changed. Their survival and progress depended upon his ability to communicate the change.

JFK crafted one of the most important messages of his life … courtesy of a coconut. He learnt the power of a succinct message that was crystal clear.

What crystal clear message do you need to craft and communicate today?

"The single biggest problem in communication is the illusion that it has taken place."

George Bernard Shaw

TAKEAWAY

PIVOTAL MOMENT

The Really Useful Appendix 30
Check out how important communication is in Kotter's eight stages of leading change.

Week 7
Be inspired

"Our chief want is someone who will inspire us to be what we know we could be."

Ralph Waldo Emerson

The Oxford English Dictionary defines "to inspire" as to fill (someone) with the urge or ability to do or feel something.

It comes from the Latin *inspirare*, literally meaning to breathe or blow into. It had religious origins of "breathing in the Spirit".

This week you have the opportunity for some great pivotal moments where you can "breathe-in" and be inspired.

We are going to take in some lessons from a fiction writer, a woman in a wheelchair, some Sudanese tribesmen, a footballer and a chauffeur. Inspiration can come from some unlikely sources. Look to be inspired.

If you are not inspired, don't expect your people to be.

DAY 31

Follow your ideas

LITTLE CHANCE OF MAKING MONEY

The idea came to her while she sat on her delayed train. It inspired her.

It was 1990 and J. K. Rowling was a researcher and bilingual secretary for Amnesty International. She decided to put her idea about a certain Harry Potter into writing. In 1991 she moved to Portugal to teach English. She met her first husband and had a daughter, but the couple split up so J. K. Rowling returned to the UK and moved to Edinburgh. The next few years were tough – she was a single parent relying on state benefits and worked on the book while her daughter slept. But her finished manuscript was rejected by 12 publishers and she was told that she had little chance of making money through writing children's books.

Rowling owes much to an eight-year-old girl. Alice Newton was the daughter of chairman of the publishers, Bloomsbury. Alice was given the first chapter of Harry Potter to review by her father. She loved it and immediately demanded the next chapter.

In June 1997, *Harry Potter and the Philosopher's Stone* was published. *Harry Potter* became the best-selling book series in history, generating over £500m revenues. J. K. Rowling had pursued her idea for seven years without the encouragement or any hint of the rewards it would bring.

Ideas inspire.

Follow your ideas.

And what will you pursue without guarantee of success?

For many people their inspiration is found outside of their day job, but that can't be the case for the business leader – otherwise move over, as you are taking somebody's place.

Inspiration, nevertheless, can run dry and motivation can wane. Think again about what you believe in. Why not start to feed it and pursue it again? Then watch your energy levels increase.

"Leadership is the art of giving people a platform for spreading ideas that work."

Seth Godin

TAKEAWAY

PIVOTAL MOMENT

The Really Useful Appendix 31
Try out the Brick and Blanket test with your team to make the most of your ideas.

DAY 32

Be an inspiration

IN MEMORY OF DORIS

Whom do you most admire?

For over 25 years I have surveyed business leaders, asking them whom they admire.

Those who are regularly listed include Nelson Mandela, Bill Gates, Stephen Hawking and Richard Branson. Each with their own remarkable story of success – a freedom fighter who became President , the supreme "nerd" who transformed how we do business, a man with a remarkable intellect who has become pre-eminent in his field despite terrible disability and a buccaneering, serial entrepreneur who left school at 16.

The 2015 YouGov poll of the "most admired women" contains an equally diverse group. Angelina Jolie, Malala Yousafzai, Hillary Clinton, Queen Elizabeth 2nd and Michelle Obama headed the list.

One of the most inspirational people I have known was at the complete opposite end of the spectrum - an unknown, a "non-achiever". Doris Allen was brought up in a deprived area of London. Following the birth of her only son, Doris developed rheumatoid arthritis and had to use a wheelchair. For the final 50 years of her life she was completely dependent upon others to feed and care for her. But Doris inspired me and many other people because she never seemed confined by the mundanity of life. Her daily watchword was "count your blessings". She ran her race, with character undiminished.

Who stands out in your world? What characterises them?

How can you inspire those around you to be what they could be?

Be an inspiration. It's good to be inspired.

"And in the end it's not the years in your life that count. It's the life in your years."

Abraham Lincoln

TAKEAWAY

PIVOTAL MOMENT

The Really Useful Appendix 32
Let former circus clown Derek Sivers inspire you to follow stand-out people.

DAY 33

Actions communicate and engage others

MUD AIRSTRIPS

Whilst at university I received a lesson in leadership that I am still learning.

My summer of voluntary work consisted of employing some 70 local tribesmen in the Southern Sudan. We maintained and extended mud airstrips which were critical for medical supplies. I was a total novice with the task at hand, the language and the culture. I was not exactly well qualified for the job.

On the first day my early attempt to "speak the language" nearly ended in disaster. I wanted to welcome them but I mistakenly said, in Dinka, to my group of workers "Greetings, there is *no* work today". I didn't understand why they looked so disappointed, then turned around and started to leave!

I had to learn other ways to communicate. Sign language, smiling and laughing became very important. My top learning was that "actions speak louder than words."

We developed a great camaraderie. It peaked for me on the last day when, to my astonishment, they sang a song of thanks to me. It was a humbling, but unforgettable moment. I was in no doubt who gained most from the experience.

Communication is key to successful leadership. I learned that communication is not just about speech. Actions communicate and engage others...

Ella Fitzgerald's song has a similar theme:

"But this is one thing you ought to know…

Oh 't ain't what you do it's the way that you do it

… That's what gets results"

How would others describe "the way that you do it"?

"An ounce of practice is worth more than tons of preaching."

Mahatma Gandhi

TAKEAWAY

PIVOTAL MOMENT

The Really Useful Appendix 33
Look at the Transactional Analysis model to work out how you communicate with important people in your life.

DAY 34

Leadership is 24/7

THERE IS NO MISTAKE

The day the paparazzi missed.

A very good friend of mine was lunching in a restaurant in Alderley Edge, a smart town just south of Manchester where many footballers have their mansions. He was engaged in a deep conversation with a friend, but was disturbed by loud laughter from a table full of lads.

My friend went over to the neighbouring table and politely asked if they would mind quietening down or moving to another part of the restaurant. Not quite knowing what their reaction would be, he was relieved when they immediately apologised and moved elsewhere. His conversation continued in peace.

As the dessert dishes were being taken away and he was ordering coffee he asked for the bill. The waiter returned with the coffees and said the bill had already been paid. My friend thought that there must be some mistake. The waiter replied, "There is no mistake, sir. Mr David Beckham paid the bill when he left ten minutes ago."

Whether you are a leader in sport or business, what you do when nobody is looking is the real measure of your character. Leadership is 24/7.

I recently posed a simple question to 40 leaders in business, education, the arts and sport: "What has been the best leadership advice you have received?"

Fifty per cent of the responses highlighted the primary importance of the leader's character and example. Leadership is seen not heard.

Which do you want to do first: work on the example you set or ask your team to improve theirs?

> *"Real integrity is doing the right thing, knowing that nobody's going to know whether you did it or not."*
> Oprah Winfrey

TAKEAWAY

PIVOTAL MOMENT

The Really Useful Appendix 34
Find out the "surprising truth" about what really motivates people from business writer Dan Pink.

DAY 35

Try something new

THE CHAUFFEUR

The apocryphal story goes something like this ...

Albert Einstein was travelling across the USA explaining his new Theory of Relativity to university audiences. His chauffeur, Igor, drove him from Yale and to the final destination - Harvard.

As they approached, Einstein said to Igor, "You've heard my talk many times and how I've answered every question. I think you that you could even deliver this talk instead of me, Igor."

And that is what they decided to do. The Harvard audience, in this pre-internet age, didn't know what this new scientist looked like, but knew that he probably had a funny accent.

Igor was word-perfect and expertly answered every query. As he was about to finish somebody asked a complex question that had never been asked before. All eyes were on Igor.

Without a flicker, Igor said, "That may appear to be a difficult question, but is so easy that even my chauffeur could answer it," as he pointed to Einstein dressed in his chauffeur's uniform.

It's a risk to let someone take your place when you are the expert.

Management may be a science, but leadership is an art – it requires judgement and instinct. Try something - take a risk and be prepared to fail. When you put your trust in someone else it is a risk – but it also truly inspires. Nothing ventured, nothing gained.

Why not take a risk and do something new today? What will it be?

"Before you are a leader success is all about growing yourself. When you are a leader success is all about growing others."

Jack Welch

TAKEAWAY

PIVOTAL MOMENT

The Really Useful Appendix 35
What is your appetite for risk? Work out your "risk profile".

Week 8
Your life

"We thought we had the answers, it was the questions we had wrong."

Bono

Leadership extends beyond the day job. This week take time to think about your life as a whole - private, public and professional - and the choices that you want to make.

I have surveyed thousands of business leaders over 25 years, asking them, "What three changes would you like to make in your life?"

The overwhelming No.1 response has been "A better work/life balance." Curiously no- one ever responded with "Spend more time at the office."

We have created The Life Direction Wheel in The Really Useful Appendix. We hope that it may prompt you to ask questions that you may not have had time to ask yourself recently.

DAY 36

Follow your calling

EBOLA

"It's really good to be back."

Will Pooley continued, "I never meant to leave Sierra Leone. I didn't want to go, so being back feels like I'm back where I should be. I feel like I'm doing a worthwhile job... I'm a nurse and this is where they need nurses."

As the Ebola virus started to devastate Sierra Leone, Will Pooley travelled to work at a hospice in the capital, Freetown. Ebola has fearsome symptoms - high fever and massive internal bleeding. It kills as many as 90% of people it infects. Pooley went straight to the epicentre to help, but became infected himself.

He was flown back to the UK where he recovered. However, he made the headlines again when he immediately flew back to Sierra Leone to carry on the same gruelling work.

His parents were asked why their son would return and how they cope. Surprisingly, they didn't express worry but rather pride that Will had found something he loved and which made such a difference.

"If he was here he would tell you that he was made to do it."

Many people feel they are "made to do" jobs they don't enjoy or value; here is a man choosing to do a job that clearly could cost him his life.

Are you "made to do it" because of the demands of your boss or your bank balance ... or are you "made to do it" because that is who you are?

Find out what you are made to do. Follow your calling.

"Don't ask yourself what the world needs – ask yourself what makes you come alive, and then go do it. Because what the world needs is people who have come alive."

Harold Thurman Whitman

TAKEAWAY

PIVOTAL MOMENT

The Really Useful Appendix 36
Read a short introduction to The Life Direction Wheel and then examine your core vision, values and goals.

DAY 37

A life of integrity is unsinkable

THE TITANIC MISTAKE

Unsinkable!

The *Titanic* was the largest ship afloat. As she set sail on her maiden voyage from Southampton to New York City she was considered unsinkable because of new buoyancy technology. Her hull was divided into sixteen watertight compartments. It was thought that up to four of these compartments could be damaged or even flooded, and the ship would stay afloat.

In the early morning of 15 April 1912 the *Titanic* collided with an iceberg and it sank, with the loss of over 1,500 lives.

On 1 September 1985 the wreck of the *Titanic* was found intact lying on the ocean floor. Previously it had been thought that the hull must have been ripped apart by the iceberg. But there was no sign of a long gash. What they discovered was that damage to one compartment had indeed affected all the rest.

James Cameron, producer of the movie Titanic, says, "The *Titanic* is a metaphor of life. We are all on the *Titanic*."

Our "titanic mistake" may be to try to compartmentalise our lives.

Of course we have different roles in life which demand different approaches from us. But some things should be undivided.

A definition of integrity is "The state of being complete or whole"

Integrity cannot be kept in just one compartment of your life. It has to permeate the whole. Only one small hole below the waterline can sink the ship. A life of integrity is whole and undivided - it's unsinkable.

What do you want to ensure is whole and undivided in your life?

"It takes 20 years to build a reputation and five minutes to ruin it. Think about that and you'll do things differently."
Warren Buffett

TAKEAWAY

PIVOTAL MOMENT

The Really Useful Appendix 37
Continue with The Life Direction Wheel to clarify and establish your hopes.

DAY 38

Put first things first

RAIN OR SNOW

I looked across the field and there was Dad clapping.

I didn't think it was that unusual that my Dad watched every sporting match or race that I was in. I thought that was just what Dads do.

He had a very demanding job, on the board of the Financial Times, yet he would arrange his work to fit in with me and my sporting schedule. I wasn't even that good, but I know I did much better than I would have done because Dad was there. For ten years, rain or snow, regardless of train trouble or bad traffic, he was there.

Once I started working and couldn't even get away at 6pm, I started to wonder how he managed to do it. I found myself rushing around and crises seemed to pop up just as I wanted to leave. However, my children are now in teams and guess what? I'm not going to miss their games.

The fact that I was such a priority for my Dad has given me confidence. His investment has truly paid dividends in my life. I remember the journeys home and I can picture him on the touch line even now. I want the same for my children, so I've made that a priority. It doesn't seem important now, but in ten years it will bear fruit.

And maybe in 20 years' time, my kids will watch all their kids' matches.

What are you prioritising today that will bear fruit in five or ten years' time?

"What you leave behind is not what is engraved in stone monuments, but what is woven into the lives of others."

Pericles

TAKEAWAY

PIVOTAL MOMENT

The Really Useful Appendix 38
Address some big questions about "doing stuff with others".

DAY 39

Leave the legacy you want

BURIED IN THE RUBBLE

The bomb exploded.

It was 8th November 1987. The IRA had detonated a bomb in Enniskillen, Northern Ireland, killing 11 people and injuring 64.

Gordon Wilson and his daughter, Marie, were buried in rubble. Unable to move, he held her hand and comforted her as she lay dying.

Her last words were, "Daddy, I love you very much."

The BBC later described the bombing as a turning point in the troubles. Pivotal to the change in attitude towards this sort of attack was Wilson's reaction to the death of his daughter.

In an interview with the BBC, Wilson said, "I bear no ill will. I bear no grudge. Dirty sort of talk is not going to bring her back to life. She was a great wee lassie. She loved her profession. She was a pet. She's dead. She's in heaven and we shall meet again. I will pray for these men tonight and every night."

As historian Jonathan Bardon recounts, "No words in more than 25 years of violence in Northern Ireland had such a powerful, emotional impact."

Subsequently, the IRA issued a statement offering "sincerest condolences and apologies" for his daughter's death. In 1989 Wilson helped launch a community outreach programme entitled the Spirit of Enniskillen Trust which helped young people in Northern Ireland participate in international programmes and gave bursaries to promote reconciliation in Northern Ireland.

Leave the legacy you want.

What would be left behind now if you moved on at work or home?

"The ultimate measure of a man is not where he stands in times of comfort, but where he stands at times of challenge and controversy."

Martin Luther King Jr

TAKEAWAY

PIVOTAL MOMENT

The Really Useful Appendix 39
Take a fresh look at your career, how you want to develop it
and the legacy you would like to leave.

DAY 40

Keep on going

10,000 WAYS THAT WON'T WORK

"Your Tommy is too stupid to learn. We cannot have him at our school".

Thomas, aged four, gave the note to his mother. He'd just been sent home from school. Young Tommy was something of a dreamer. If there had been a school psychologist he would probably have been diagnosed with attention deficit disorder.

If you are a parent, with normal aspirations for your child, this is a letter that would either make you fume or cry, or both. This would not be the last setback young Tommy would face – there would be 10,000 more.

Tommy – or Thomas Edison, as he became better known - knew about setbacks. He famously failed in his quest to produce an electric light bulb 10,000 times before he finally succeeded. Or as he put it:

"I have not failed. I've just found 10,000 ways that won't work."

He knew how to dream, but also not to give up in the face of disappointment. Edison went on to have over 2,000 patents to his name. His many inventions have transformed our modern world.

When something doesn't work out, it's important to face the reality but not lose sight of the fact that there are other ways forward. Leaders are dealers in *truth*, but are also dealers in *hope*.

Psychologist Martin Seligman, in his book *Learned Optimism*, highlights that the pessimist, when facing a difficulty, is likely to believe that bad events will last a long time. The optimist, in the same circumstance, believes that defeat is just a temporary setback.

Think of a setback. One that was important. And go again - and keep on going,

"I'd rather be a comma than a full stop."
Coldplay

TAKEAWAY

PIVOTAL MOMENT

The Really Useful Appendix 40
Take stock of what you have been doing over that last 40
days and capture what you want to take forward.

Section C
THE REALLY USEFUL APPENDIX

"Essentially, all models are wrong, but some are useful."
George E.P. Box

Those people who have had their appendix removed will tell you that it was of no use and that they are better without it! Most people think that is the same with a book appendix.

We have tried to be a bit different and make this appendix useful – hopefully, really useful – to you.

It has been designed to be a natural follow-up to each of the 40 Days. We are sharing ideas and frameworks that you can easily apply to everyday leadership situations. Some are well known, and in common usage, and others we have created. They are intended to be practical and to be used – so keep your pen or pencil out. We hope that you will still be referring to some of them way into the future.

Usually each day will be stand-alone, but in Weeks 5 and 8 the themes continue throughout the whole week.

Before the 40 Days start there are two frameworks that we hope will set the context for your role and personal style.

Have fun working with them.

SoaP: Strategy-on-a-Page

1) VISION	What is your big aspiration? What is the purpose of your enterprise?	• Best service in town • Our product in every US home • Education for all in Africa
2) VALUES	What are your top three golden rules?	• Customer comes first • Think different • Care for colleagues
3) GOALS	What will success look like? What are the top three longer term results you want?	• Win the league • Smile ten times a day • Make 20% profit
4) CURRENT POSITION	Where are you on the journey? How are you performing today against your goals?	• Eighth in the league • Smiling twice a day • 3% profit
5) OPPORTUNITIES	What will help you progress? What are your three biggest opportunities?	• Buy a new player • Open new store • Invest in coaching
6) RISKS	What may hold you back? What are your two greatest risks?	• Lose staff • Bad delivery
7) NEXT STEPS	What are your three mid-term priorities?	• Win five more customers • Set up charity event • Reduce electric bills

Complete your own SoaP on the next page.

Each point should be "tweetable" - no more than 140 characters.

SoaP: Strategy-on-a-Page

1) VISION	What is your big aspiration? What is the purpose of your enterprise?	
2) VALUES	What are your top three golden rules?	
3) GOALS	What will success look like? What are the top three longer term results you want?	
4) CURRENT POSITION	Where are you on the journey? How are you performing today against your goals?	
5) OPPORTUNITIES	What will help you progress? What are your three biggest opportunities?	
6) RISKS	What may hold you back? What are your two greatest risks?	
7) NEXT STEPS	What are your three mid-term priorities?	

Assess your approach to navigate as a leader

What is your natural style when you need to: see the big picture; choose the right direction; do the right things; check progress; and be inspired?

Circle *three* words in *each* box – or use other words - which most reflect your style. Choose words you really identify with and that describe your *most dominant characteristics*.

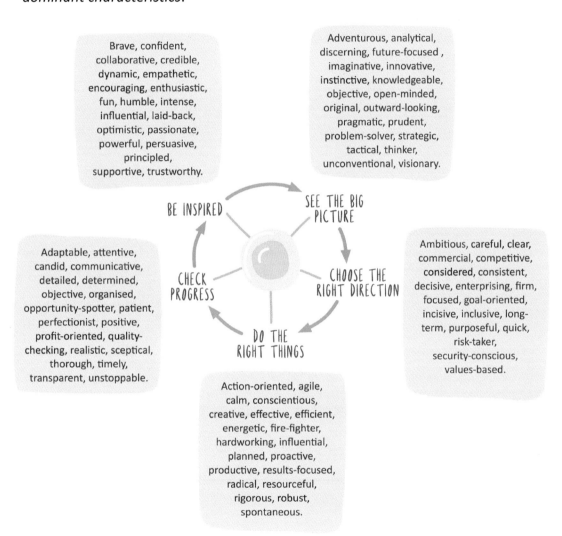

Prioritise your traits (number them 1 to 15). Where are your dominant characteristics positioned? Where are you less strong?

Think about what you have to offer others and what you will need to draw on from others.

DAY 1

The GROW model

All learning involves change. If you're not changing, you can't be improving. As you embark on 40 days of self-coaching, how are you going to change? Not all learning is planned, but the GROW model can help you plan your growth.

Most coaching focuses on the following areas:

 <u>G</u>oal – Where are you trying to get to? What are you trying to achieve?

 current <u>R</u>eality – Where are you now? What are your challenges and opportunities?

 <u>O</u>ptions – What possibilities enable you to achieve your goal from your current reality? Bear in mind it won't be a straight line.

 <u>W</u>ill – What choice(s) are you going to make, and how willing are you to see this through?

Use GROW now to start your 40 Days growth plan. Don't forget 'W', which turns good intentions into action.

Adapted from Sir John Whitmore

DAY 2

The Four Circles

What you believe will guide your career. What do you think the "world needs"? What do you really "love doing"? If you can answer those questions it will help you find your vocation and purpose.

For example, the world *needed* Nelson Mandela's battle to overcome apartheid. He *loved* the cause, was *great* at it and therefore was a man who was *passionate* about his *mission* and *purpose*. Later, he was *paid* for it, giving him a *profession* and *vocation*.

Plot all the different talents and leadership roles you have on this chart.

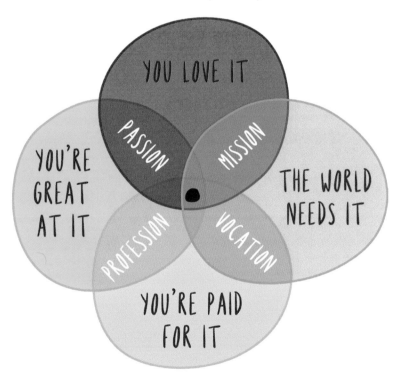

(Author unknown)

DAY 3

What are your best cards?

You can only "play the cards" you have … but you can improve the way you play the game.

What are your three best cards? Write down your top three strengths that will help you and your team to win. Highlight how you could play each card more effectively.

What other "good, but not great" cards do you have that you could play more wisely? Highlight two "lesser strengths" and state how you can improve them.

What card don't you have, but you need to succeed? Who could provide you with that card or strength? How are you going to get it?

DAY 4

Greek Temple model of leadership

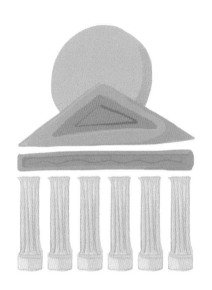

Four critical roles of your business

PURPOSE: The temple (your business) is positioned towards the sun (your customer).

DIRECTION: The triangular pediment points towards the sun. All you do is focused on the customer.

CONNECTION: The horizontal lintel ensures that the whole building is connected.

EXPERTISE: The vertical columns give the building height and represent the range of expertise you offer your customer.

The shape of your leadership role

A. Build the expertise to help your customer thrive and prosper.

B. Be T-shaped … make the right connections to join up your business.

C. Set direction and priorities. Be the visible arrow-head.

D. Position your whole enterprise towards the right customers, to fulfil its purpose.

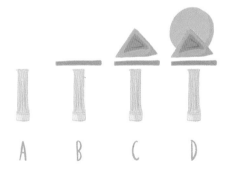

What is the shape of your current leadership style?

What will it need to look like?

DAY 5

Daniel Goleman – Leadership Styles

We all have natural leadership styles. Our natural style(s) works best in some situations, but not all. The most effective leaders adapt their style to meet the need of the situation. Daniel Goleman identified six leadership styles associated with different aspects of emotional intelligence and all useful in different situations.

What are your preferred styles? Rank them 1-6. Ask some people who know you well to rank your preferred styles. Are their rankings the same as yours?

	1) COERCIVE	2) AUTHORITATIVE	3) AFFILIATIVE
The leader's modus operandi	Demands immediate compliance	Mobilises people toward a vision	Creates harmony and builds emotional bonds
The style in a phrase	"Do what I tell you"	"Come with me"	"People come first"
When the style works best	In a crisis, to kick start a turnaround, or with problem employees	When changes require a new vision, or when a clear direction is needed	To heal rifts in a team or to motivate people during stressful circumstances
Impact on climate	Negative	Strongly positive	Positive
Rank 1-6			

	4) DEMOCRATIC	5) PACESETTING	6) COACHING
The leader's modus operandi	Forges consensus through participation	Sets high standards for performance	Develops people for the future
The style in a phrase	"What do you think?"	"Do as I do, now"	"Try this"
When the style works best	To build buy-in or consensus, or to get input from valuable employees	To get quick results from highly motivated and competent people	To help an employee improve performance or develop long-term strengths
Impact on climate	Positive	Negative	Positive
Rank 1-6			

How can you play to your strengths? Do you need to develop other styles? How might you work on this?

DAY 6

Hiring for success

Use the Hiring for Success Chart to:

- define and rank the success criteria for your next hire

- prepare questions

- rank the candidate against the *success criteria* not qualifications

- record your decision and comments

ROLE:	CANDIDATE:	
WHAT ARE THE 7 SUCCESS CRITERIA IN PRIORITY ORDER?	QUESTIONS	SCORE: 1 — 5
1)		
2)		
3)		
4)		
5)		
6)		
7)		
DECISIONS & COMMENTS		

Select your team on the basis of the fit of character (personality and values), competence (expertise to deliver) and chemistry (get-on-ability).

DAY 7

Different strokes for different folks

Individuals need to be handled individually.

Think about your team members and plot where they are on the Potential/Performance grid.

Empathise with them – put yourself "in their shoes." What might be the most relevant question for each of your people?

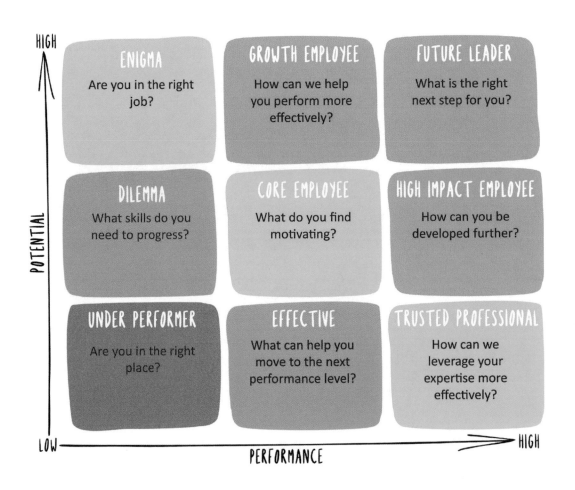

DAY 8

Engaging your people

Numerous studies by Towers Watson, Gallup and others have shown that companies with higher engagement among their staff outperform their peers. The following items emerged from Gallup's pioneering research as the best predictors of employee and workgroup performance.

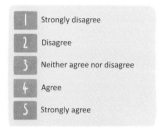

1	Strongly disagree
2	Disagree
3	Neither agree nor disagree
4	Agree
5	Strongly agree

GALLUP'S Q12	SCORE 1 — 5
STAGE 1: PRIMARY NEEDS / NEW IN ROLE	
1) I know what is expected of me at work.	
2) I have the materials and equpiment to do my work right.	
sub total	/ 10
STAGE 2: AM I VALUED? / MANAGER RELATIONSHIP	
3) At work, I have the opportunity to do what I do best everyday.	
4) In the last seven days, I have received recognition or praise for good work.	
5) My supervisor, or someone at work, seems to care about me as a person.	
6) There is someone at work who encourages my development.	
sub total	/ 20
STAGE 3: DO I BELONG?	
7) At work, my opinions seem to count.	
8) The mission of my company makes me feel that my job is important.	
9) My associates or colleagues are committed to doing quality work.	
10) I have a best friend at work.	
sub total	/ 20
STAGE 4: AM I LEARNING AND GROWING?	
11) In the past six months someone has spoken to me about my progress.	
12) This last year, I have had opportunities at work to learn and grow.	
sub total	/ 10
total	/ 60

The four stages are sequential steps to engagement. Complete the twelve questions and total your engagement score at each stage. Ask your colleagues to score their engagement. Which three areas do you need or want to work on? What can you do to change your score?

DAY 9

Boosting confidence

Assess your team members' levels of confidence. Score each individual on a 1 (low) – 5 (high) scale in relation to their confidence to make decisions, achieve in tasks, engage with people effectively or to move forward and "do more".

Talk with them. Together identify practical ways to boost confidence. Devise targeted ways to support, coach, challenge, and stretch them.

TEAM MEMBER SCORE:

1	No evidence
3	Competent
5	Outstanding

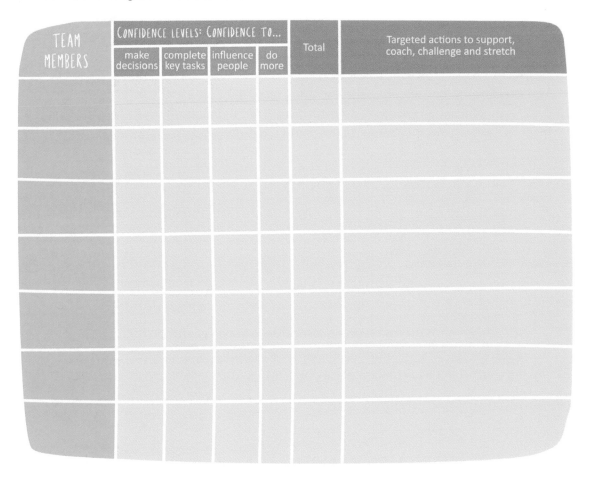

TEAM MEMBERS	CONFIDENCE LEVELS: CONFIDENCE TO...				Total	Targeted actions to support, coach, challenge and stretch
	make decisions	complete key tasks	influence people	do more		

DAY 10

Patrick Lencioni – The Five Dysfunctions of a Team

Patrick Lencioni, in his book *The Five Dysfunctions of a Team*, identifies five factors in dysfunctional teams. Improving team performance requires a focus on these five areas:

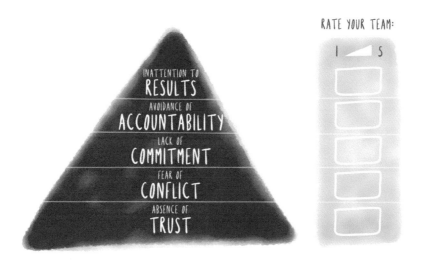

Trust: Trust starts with every person wanting to achieve team goals above personal goals. No ego.

Conflict: Trust allows honest dialogue. From constructive conflict the best solutions emerge.

Commitment: Constructive conflict allows everyone to have their say. So everyone is able to commit to the team decision.

Accountability: From this mutual commitment everyone is prepared to hold each other to account.

Results: Accountability means reviewing performance openly, creating the right environment for high performance.

Rate your team between 1 and 5 against each factor, starting with 'Trust' (1 = 'low trust' and 5 = 'high trust', and so on). What do you need to work on?

Adapted from "The Five Dysfunctions of a Team" by Patrick Lencioni. See *www.tablegroup.com* for more tools.

DAY 11

Clarity and Confidence

How clear and confident are your team about the strategy?

Ask your each of team to place an "X" on the chart showing how clear and confident they are about the strategy. You may want to allow them to mark their Xs anonymously.

How many of the team are in the top right hand quadrant and therefore confident in, and clear about, the strategy?

A 2013 McKinsey study of 772 Board Directors reported that only:

- 34% thought that their Board understood their strategy

- 22% thought their Board understood how their business created value

- 16% thought their Board understood the dynamics of their industry

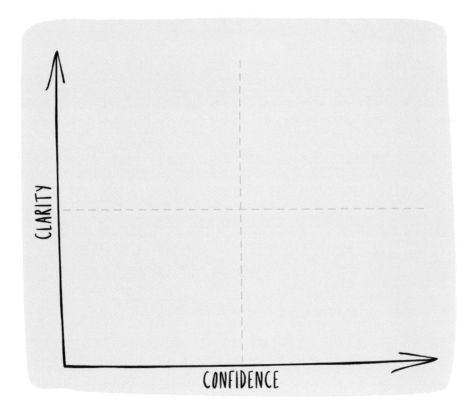

(Author unknown)

DAY 12

Your solar system

Work out your own solar system.

Who are the ten most important people in your solar system?

Select five people from outside (orange) and five from inside (green) your organisation. Write their name and their top priority in a circle.

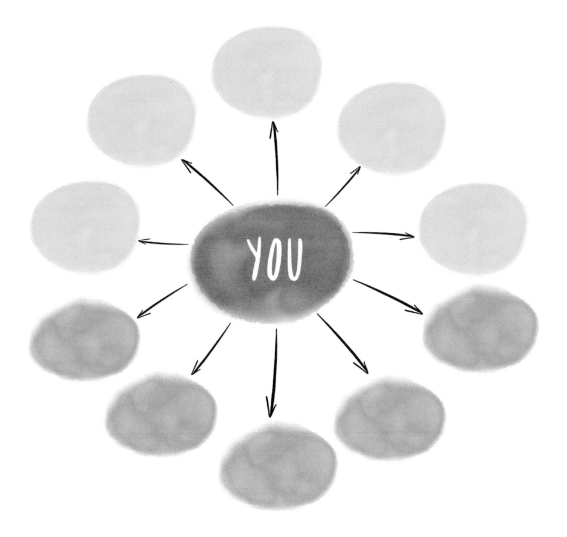

What are you going to do to improve the engagement and the alignment of the 10 key people in your solar system?

DAY 13

The "Trusted Adviser"

To be an effective leader, one of the critical roles you will need to develop and keep working on is being a Trusted Adviser, particularly in relation to your customers and stakeholders.

Why not ask your customers for some feedback about what is going well and what could be improved?

Adapt the following survey to suit your needs and guarantee their anonymity.

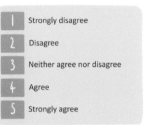

1	Strongly disagree
2	Disagree
3	Neither agree nor disagree
4	Agree
5	Strongly agree

	Please let me know how you think I'm doing as your adviser. Do you think I am...	SCORE 1 — 5
1)	In it for a long term relationship, not short term gain?	
2)	Putting your interests in front of my own?	
3)	Genuinely interested in you and your business?	
4)	Not a "yes person" and I work hard to understand your underlying issues?	
5)	Reliable and do what I say I will do?	
6)	An expert in my field?	
7)	Enjoyable to work with?	
8)	Passionate?	
9)	Authentic?	
	total	/ 45

Adapted from David Maister, author of *The Trusted Advisor.*

DAY 14

Co-consultancy

Co-consultancy is a structured approach to teams working together to solve problems and create opportunities – in a limited time.

One person in the group (the 'client') explains the issue to their colleagues (the 'co-consultants'), one of whom also takes responsibility to facilitate the process and keep time.

	PROCESS	RULES	PURPOSE	TIME
1	Client explains the problem	• Co-consultants silent	Client defines the problem as clearly as possible	2 mins
2	Co-consultants explore the issue through Q&A	• Questions only • Client answers briefly	Co-consultants understand problem clearly	3 mins
3	Co-consultants offer solutions	• Client silent, takes notes • No judgement on ideas	Co-consultants generate as many solutions as possible	5 mins
4	Client explores solutions through Q&A	• Questions only • Co-consultants answer briefly	Client understands possible solutions fully	3 mins
5	Client decides on and explains their plan	• Co-consultants silent	Client owns decision and takes action	1 min

Why not use this with your team to unblock a seemingly intractable problem, or make the most of new opportunities?

(Author unknown)

DAY 15

The Big Health Check

How healthy are you and your team at work?

Mark where you are on the Challenge Line below. The questions refer to your work, but can be applied to many aspects of your life.

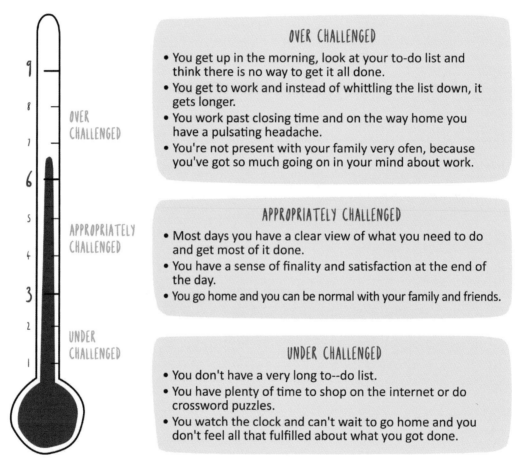

OVER CHALLENGED
- You get up in the morning, look at your to-do list and think there is no way to get it all done.
- You get to work and instead of whittling the list down, it gets longer.
- You work past closing time and on the way home you have a pulsating headache.
- You're not present with your family very ofen, because you've got so much going on in your mind about work.

APPROPRIATELY CHALLENGED
- Most days you have a clear view of what you need to do and get most of it done.
- You have a sense of finality and satisfaction at the end of the day.
- You go home and you can be normal with your family and friends.

UNDER CHALLENGED
- You don't have a very long to--do list.
- You have plenty of time to shop on the internet or do crossword puzzles.
- You watch the clock and can't wait to go home and you don't feel all that fulfilled about what you got done.

Where are you? Where are your team? Where would you put the whole organisation?

Bill Hybels' research indicates that:

- Your best work is done when you're slightly more than appropriately challenged (between 6 and 7 on the thermostat).

- You cannot stay dangerously over-challenged (7, 8 and 9) for too long.

- High performers will leave when under-challenged.

Adapted from Bill Hybels

DAY 16

Simon Sinek – The Golden Circle

"People don't buy what you do, they buy why you do it."

Why?

"Very few organisations know why they do what they do. 'Why' is not about making money. Making money is a result. 'Why' is a purpose, cause or belief. It's the very reason your organisation exists."

How?

"Some organisations know how they do it. These are the things that make them special or set them apart from the competition."

What?

"Every organisation knows what they do. These are the products they make or the services they offer."

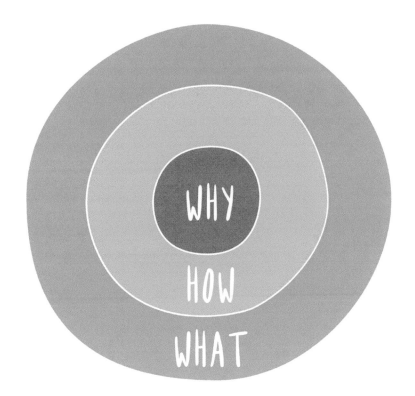

Spend a moment answering this question – why?

Adapted from *Start With Why*, by Simon Sinek

DAY 17

The Eisenhower Matrix

Everything that comes across can be measured as urgent/non-urgent and important/unimportant.

The Eisenhower Matrix, adapted below, provides a simple rule of thumb to increase your effectiveness and productivity.

Look at your 'to do' list now. What can you ditch? What can you delegate? What should you plan in your diary? What do you need to do now? Commit to it by completing the matrix.

DAY 18

Know your values

Your values are your internal navigation system – your personal compass. They are your "golden rules", your terms and conditions, which you live and work by. They dictate your priorities and decisions. Values are usually fairly stable, but as you move through life, they may change... therefore you have a choice.

Identify your internal navigation system – your set of values in your **Private** (personal, core), **Public** (family and social) and **Professional** (job and organisation) life. When have you been most happy in each of the three dimensions? Prioritise your top three values for each dimension

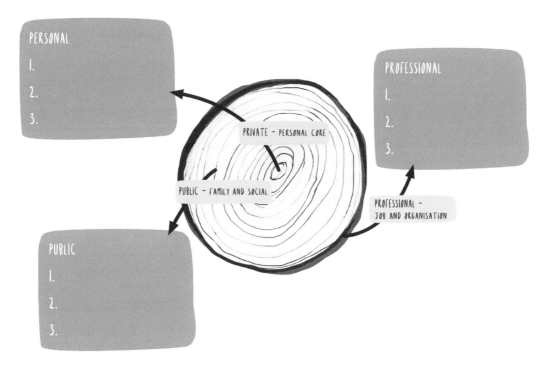

Tension occurs when your values are conflicted – either through misalignment between the three dimensions in your own life or when someone else conflicts your values. Address the tensions:

- Spot the conflict early and work out the right strategy to tackle it

- Know the hierarchy of your values

- Get the objective views of people you trust, but remember it's your choice and your responsibility

DAY 19

Ask great questions

How do you understand the expectations and motivations of others? Ask them!

The ability to ask great questions is one of the most valuable skills in a leader's toolkit … and it is one which you *can* develop. Here are three "tips and tricks" to help you understand and engage others more effectively:

1. Neil Rackham devised **SPIN questioning** to help sales people diagnose a customer's deepest needs. Rackham's approach to questioning is just as relevant to leaders. It will help you to challenge wrong assumptions and go deeper than just the symptoms. Focus more on the "I" and "N" questions. Research SPIN further to help you ask the right questions at the right time.

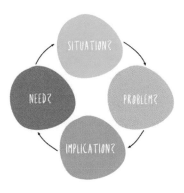

2. Play the **"Turn it into a question"** game. Every day put three question marks into your pocket. Use them to turn a statement into a question. For example, "These are our strengths…" (tell) becomes "What do you need?" or "How can we help?" (enquire and listen).

3. Read Rudyard Kipling's poem "I keep six honest serving men" about **What** and **Why** and **When** and **How** and **Where** and **Who**. How can these help you?

DAY 20

The wisdom of Steve Jobs

In 2005, Steve Jobs addressed students at Stanford University, sharing some of his philosophy of life, work and love.

Long before developing the cancer that would eventually lead to his death, Jobs used the prospect of death to give him perspective in decision making:

> *"Remembering that I'll be dead soon is the most important tool I've ever encountered to help me make the big choices in life. Because almost everything — all external expectations, all pride, all fear of embarrassment or failure — these things just fall away in the face of death, leaving only what is truly important. Remembering that you are going to die is the best way I know to avoid the trap of thinking you have something to lose."*

He spelt out the implications of this for making decisions in work, life and love:

> *"Your time is limited, so don't waste it living someone else's life."*

What would you like to be remembered for? Write your own epitaph in no more than 140 characters.

What choices or changes in direction do you need to make for it to be real?

You can hear Steve Jobs' full speech at *https://www.youtube.com/watch?v=BzEzUE5dydo*.

Week 5

Do the right things

This week the Really Useful Appendix draws on a concept that was first introduced in Leaders' Map. We call the concept GLEPS™.

GLEPS is a simple, but unique way to classify or categorise the <u>potential</u> value of everything you do.

Each of your tasks, decisions or events can fit into one of the following categories:

TRANSFORMATIVE

CREATIVE

PROACTIVE

PRODUCTIVE

REACTIVE

Each day this week we will focus on a specific value.

Start to think about the decisions you have to make, the relationships you need to initiate and deepen, the ideas you could generate and even the emails you need to write in terms of the value they add.

What is their potential – their value? Are they potentially transformative or just reactive? How creative or proactive will you need to be, or do you just need to be very productive?

Going forward you could employ the GLEPS thinking to choose what you do and how you will to do it.

DAY 21

Make transformative choices

A transformative choice or event will be high impact and could lead to radical change. It is a potential game-changer.

Reflect on the things that have had a transformational impact on your life, whether at work or home.

Think ahead to the coming days and weeks. What activities, decisions or events have the *potential* to be game-changers for you?

GLEPS	PRACTICAL EXAMPLES	MY TRANSFORMATIVE ACTIVITIES
TRANSFORMATIVE ⭐ GAME CHANGER	• Acquire a competitor • Have a baby • Hire a sales director • Start in a new market • Refinance the business	

DAY 22

Be creative

When you are being creative you are generating something new. It could be about strategy or learning or re-energising the team. You are aiming to turn on the light.

When have you been most creative? What were the benefits?

In what ways can you be creative in the future?

GLEPS	PRACTICAL EXAMPLES	MY CREATIVE ACTIVITIES
CREATIVE TURNS ON THE LIGHT	• Develop a new product • Go on a sabbatical • Write an article • Train high potential leaders • Work with your team on the marketing strategy	

DAY 23

Be proactive

Proactive tasks are when you take the initiative and anticipate the future. Being proactive enables you to spot and unlock opportunities. You are being enterprising.

In what ways do you demonstrate proactivity? What have been the results and benefits?

How would you like to be more proactive going forward?

GLEPS	PRACTICAL EXAMPLES	MY PROACTIVE ACTIVITIES
PROACTIVE BE ENTERPRISING	• Talk to your client about a new idea • Ask someone out on a date • Give your best player a rise before she asks • Offer to help your boss with her biggest problem • Suggest to your competitor that he should sell up	

DAY 24

Be productive

Being productive is about tackling core, day-to-day responsibilities. It is about getting things done. You will want to be producing your best effectively and efficiently.

Productivity gurus would say "Do it … delegate it … diarise it … or ditch it!"

What are the key productive activities that you need to tackle in the coming week?

GLEPS	PRACTICAL EXAMPLES	MY PRODUCTIVE ACTIVITIES
PRODUCTIVE PRODUCING EFFECTIVELY AND EFFICIENTLY	• Complete your team development plans • Prepare well for your customer visit • Mow the grass • Write monthly financial report • Attend operation manager's retirement party	

DAY 25

Be reactive only when you need to

It is very easy to be event-driven and become reactive. A reactive task can take you off-course and may add little value.

Being reactive, however, is not all bad as new opportunities may unexpectedly arise. Nevertheless, you still need to ask "Should I stop this activity?"

What do you need to stop?

GLEPS	PRACTICAL EXAMPLES	MY REACTIVE ACTIVITIES
REACTIVE ? SHOULD I STOP THIS ACTIVITY?	• Meet the sales rep that called unexpectedly • Try to solve your production manager's problem for him • Reply to spam • Speak at a sports club dinner you didn't want to attend	

DAY 26

Listening

Those with natural empathy are world champion listeners. They have innate "emotional intelligence". They put themselves in somebody else's shoes. They see and feel things from the perspective of others. This can often be the missing link for many an aspiring leader. Remember you can't change your wiring – your

natural empathy – but you can develop strategies that can radically alter your ability to listen.

Check out the anagram options for "Listen".

To engage or enlist others, you have to listen. To listen you will need to be silent.

Listening, however, is not passive; it is one of the most active things a leader can do. The following tips on *Becoming an Active Listener* are a précis from the excellent Mind Tools website (www.mindtools.com).

1. Pay attention: give the speaker your undivided attention and acknowledge the message	• Look at them directly • Don't mentally prepare a rebuttal!
2. Show you're listening: use gestures to convey your attention	• Nod or smile occasionally • Encourage them to continue with small verbal comments like 'yes', and 'uh huh'
3. Provide feedback: reflect what is being said and ask questions	• "What I'm hearing is," and "Sounds like you are saying," are great ways to reflect back • Summarise their comments periodically
4. Defer judgment: interrupting is a waste of time	• Allow the speaker to finish each point before asking questions
5. Respond appropriately: active listening is a model for respect and understanding	• Be candid, open and honest in your response • Treat them in a way that you think he or she would want to be treated

DAY 27

Face the facts

What is the reality of your current situation?

Only by facing the facts – however inconvenient – can you realistically plot the next stage of your journey. Take a reality check by addressing the five questions below.

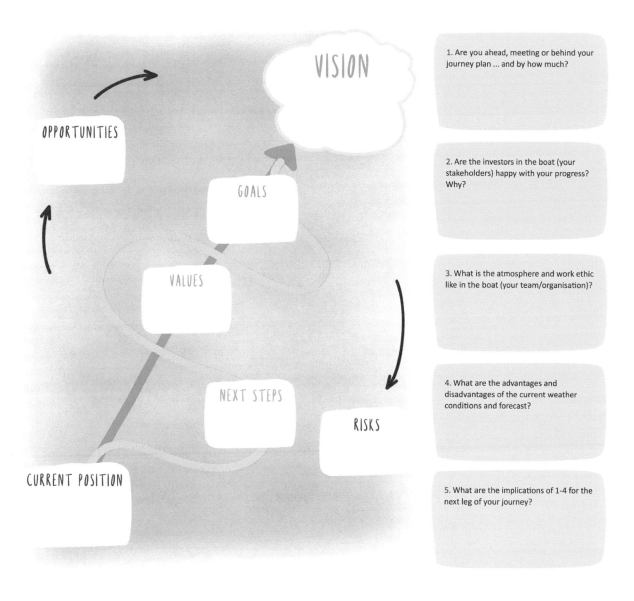

1. Are you ahead, meeting or behind your journey plan ... and by how much?

2. Are the investors in the boat (your stakeholders) happy with your progress? Why?

3. What is the atmosphere and work ethic like in the boat (your team/organisation)?

4. What are the advantages and disadvantages of the current weather conditions and forecast?

5. What are the implications of 1-4 for the next leg of your journey?

DAY 28

Bruce Tuckman - Stages of team development

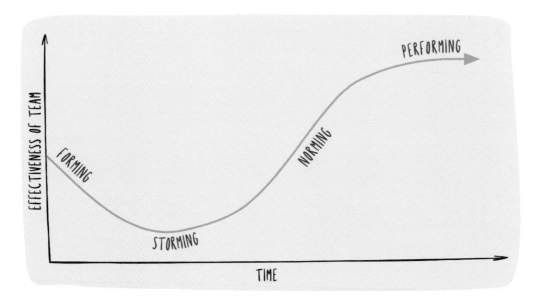

In the mid-1960s Bruce Tuckman developed his now famous team maturity model. If you haven't heard of him, you've certainly heard of his model. Each team goes through four stages of maturation:

Stage 1 – Forming: *The leader needs to direct*
The group of individuals comes together. There is lack of clarity about purpose, roles and behaviours. Performance depends on individual contributions.

Stage 2 – Storming: *The leader needs to influence and coach*
Now the individuals are shaking things up. There is conflict over all the key questions, and the answers aren't clear. Performance dips as effort is focussed inwardly.

Stage 3 – Norming: *The leader needs to involve and engage*
Then the team achieves clarity. With key questions answered, everyone is singing from the same hymn sheet. Performance improves as everyone knows their role.

Stage 4 – Performing: *The leader needs to delegate*
With all effort aligned, the team is flying! Performance soars as the sum of the team adds up to more than the sum of the individuals.

What stage is your team at? How do you need to lead to maintain or move towards high performance?

DAY 29

Belbin - Team Roles

Meredith Belbin's research showed that a successful team comprises 6-15 people and needs someone to play each of the nine roles below. People typically have two preferred roles and generally don't like to have to play other roles. If you understand your colleagues' preferred Belbin team role, you will appreciate and understand what they can contribute in teams.

Take the Belbin team assessment with the rest of your team at belbin.com.

TEAM ROLE	CONTRIBUTION	WEAKNESSES
PLANT	Creative, imaginative, free-thinking. Generates ideas and solves difficult problems	Ignores incidentals. Too preoccupied to communicate effectively
RESOURCE INVESTIGATOR	Outgoing, enthusiastic, communicative. Explores opportunities and develops contacts	Over-optimistic. Loses interest once initial enthusiasm has passed
CO-ORDINATOR	Mature, confident, identifies talent. Clarifies goals. Delegates effectively	Can be seen as manipulative. Offloads own share of work
SHAPER	Challenging, dynamic, thrives on pressure. Has the drive and courage to overcome obstacles	Prone to provocation. Offends people's feelings
MONITOR EVALUATOR	Sober, strategic, discerning. Sees all opportunities and judges accurately	Lacks drive and ability to inspire others. Can be overly critical
TEAMWORKER	Co-operative, perceptive and diplomatic. Listens and averts friction	Indecisive in crunch situations. Avoids confrontation
IMPLEMENTER	Practical, reliable, efficient. Turns ideas into action and organises work that needs to be done	Somewhat inflexible. Slow to respond to new possibilities
COMPLETER FINISHER	Painstaking, conscientious, anxious. Searches out errors. Polishes and perfects	Inclined to worry unduly. Reluctant to delegate
SPECIALIST	Single-minded, self-starting, dedicated. Provides knowledge and skills in rare supply	Contributes only on a narrow front. Dwells on technicalities

Have you got all these roles covered in your team?

DAY 30

John Kotter – Leading change

Keller and Aitken's McKinsey article *The Inconvenient Truth about Change Management* states that about 70% of change programmes fail – so you need to know why your programme will be successful!

Leading change thinker John Kotter studied many failed change programmes. He identified eight stages to change, any one of which might be the source of the failure.

	STAGE	SCORE YOUR CHANGE PROCESS 1 — 10
1)	**ESTABLISH A SENSE OF URGENCY** Why should anyone want the change? Make sure all stakeholders see benefit in the change for them or complacency will rule.	
2)	**CREATE THE GUILDING COALITION** Who will make the change happen? Successful change needs influential people not just senior people. You want no 'egos' in the team.	
3)	**DEVELOP A VISION AND STRATEGY** Only a clear vision can galvanise people's hearts and direct people's minds - clarifying thousands of decisions.	
4)	**COMMUNICATE THE CHANGE VISION** Once you've communicated the vision, do it again... and again. Model the message.	
5)	**EMPOWER EMPLOYEES FOR BROAD BASED ACTION** Allow a thousand flowers to bloom! Get rid of obstacles to change, encourage risk taking and provide training. Confront the people who say it can't happen or shouldn't happen.	
6)	**GENERATE SHORT TERM WINS** Plan for small change that is visible and clearly related to the change effort. Reward everyone involved. Small celebrations for small victories.	
7)	**CONSOLIDATE GAINS AND PRODUCE MORE CHANGE** Don't be seduced into thinking you've won the battle at this stage - keep going. Expand change into more resistant areas. Hire, promote and develop people who can implement the change vision.	
8)	**ANCHOR NEW APPROACHES IN THE CULTURE** It ain't done until it can't be reversed! Keep making the change until the new way simply becomes 'the way we do things around here.'	

What do you need to do to make sure your change programme is one of the 30% that succeed?

DAY 31

Brick and Blanket test

In the 1920s a psychology professor at Stamford, Lewis Terman, gathered a group of students with IQs over 140 and followed them through school and later life. The students were outstandingly successful at school, but only averagely successful in later life. Two students who were rejected from his group on the basis of their IQs went on to win Nobel prizes as adults.

Intellect is only one dimension of the qualities required to succeed in life. Creativity or divergent thinking is another. The brick and blanket test was first developed by the English psychologist Liam Hudson in the 1960s following another experiment tracking the success of school students.

If Terman had combined this test with IQ, his results might have been different.

Now you try it. Write down all the uses that you can think of for the brick and the blanket.

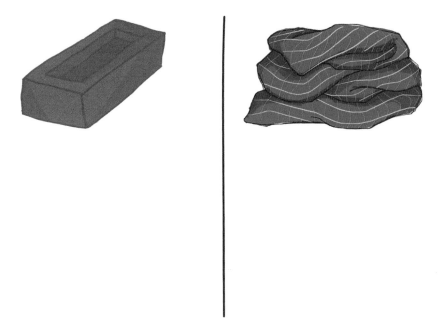

How can you and your team squeeze most out of the ideas that you already have in your business? Use this fun test as a "warm-up" to stretch your thinking and imagination.

DAY 32

Derek Sivers - How to start a movement

What transforms a lone nut into a leader?

Their first follower!

Watch Derek Sivers' three minute TED.com presentation on how to start a movement (www.ted.com/talks/derek_sivers_how_to_start_a_movement).

Sivers shows it takes guts to be the first follower. It's an underrated form of leadership in itself.

In the most important thing you're doing, are you…

...a lone nut?!

...the first follower?

...an early adopter?

...part of the crowd, looking on?

Where do you need to be?

If you're the lone nut, leading where no-one is (yet) following…

1. Have the guts to do what you do – don't be afraid of ridicule.

2. Embrace your first follower as an equal. Bear in mind future followers will follow them, not you. They will show others how to follow.

If you've found a lone nut doing something good, says Sivers…

1. "Have the guts to be the first one to stand up and join in."

2. "Have the courage to follow and show others how to follow"

DAY 33

Transactional Analysis

Transactional Analysis was developed by psychiatrist Dr Eric Berne to describe how people relate and behave towards each other – with applications in all aspects of life, work and relationships. We all have multiple facets to our personalities, characterised by Berne as 'Parent', 'Child' and 'Adult'.

The 'Parent' represents everything we have been *taught* through authority figures.

The 'Child' represents everything that we *feel*, our emotions.

The 'Adult' represents our *thoughts* and choices.

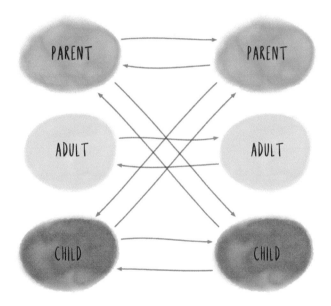

In any interaction, we can respond as a parent (seeking to dictate or coerce) or as a child (feeling disempowered, out of control) or as an adult (thinking and choosing for ourselves).

The healthiest relationships tend to be 'adult to adult' relationships.

Think of three key relationships in your life – at home, in work and perhaps elsewhere.

How would you characterise them? If necessary, how can you develop a more adult/adult relationship here?

DAY 34

What really motivates us?

There is now substantial evidence proving what does and does not motivate and inspire us.

Money does not motivate us. Economists from MIT, University of Chicago and Carnegie Mellon carried out studies in the USA and India. The studies gave people tasks which required more than rudimentary cognitive skills and then offered low, medium and high rewards based on performance. The large rewards led to poor performance. These types of carrot and stick programmes only work for basic mechanical tasks where "you do this, and you get that".

Whilst you need to pay people enough to take money off the table there are actually three factors that the science proves lead to better performance:

1. Autonomy: You need to trust that people are going to do something clever and get out of the way - give them some autonomy. Autonomy is our desire to be self-directed in our work. Some companies allow employees to do whatever they want for one day a quarter, so long as they share the results with the company. They've found an extraordinary number of fixes and innovations have come from that time.

2. Mastery: Mastery is our desire to get good at things we like. It's what makes us play musical instruments at the weekend when we won't get paid. It's what inspires people to contribute to Wikipedia and Linux for free. These are highly able people, who have paid jobs, giving hours of time for free. Why? The desire for mastery.

3. Purpose: More and more organisations are looking for a purpose beyond profit. We recognise that when the profit motive is separated from the purpose motive, bad things start to happen – unethical things, poor products, lame services and uninspiring places to work. Organisations need a purpose, beyond profit and shareholder value. The vision of Trussell Trust, who have set up over 400 Food Banks in the UK feeding one million people, is "To end hunger and poverty in the UK."

Watch: Dan Pink "The surprising truth about what motivates us" on YouTube.

DAY 35

Appetite for risk

"Nothing ventured, nothing gained". Leaders have to take risks – with people, customers, ideas and investments. The entrepreneur is well over to the left on the risk profile (based on the idea of the diffusion of innovation), the bureaucrat is to the right.

What is your appetite for risk?

Plot where you are … and where you would like to be.

How will you bridge the gap?

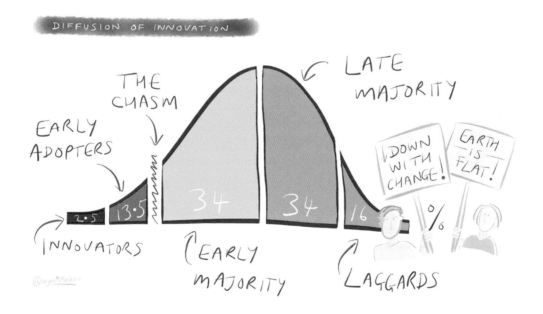

Week 8

The Life Direction Wheel

The final week of the programme is focused on the whole of life and not just your "day job."

To help you look at the whole we have created The Life Direction Wheel.

We have structured it so that you can see that the key segments of your life should fit around and be in line with your life vision, values and goals.

The Life Direction Wheel is designed to help you crystallise and articulate your choices and intentions in the three aspects of your life:

- Private (individual)

- Public (social)

- Professional (work)

Your private life involves your character, your inner being or spiritual life. It covers what you want to achieve and learn and what resources you want to build up.

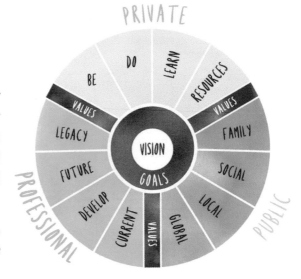

Your public life is about family, friendships, community and the wider world.

Your professional life comprises not only your job, but how you want to develop, how you want to progress in your career and what you want to pass on to others.

Using The Life Direction Wheel, the following tables will help you think through what you want in each dimension of your life.

Start with a long-term perspective, clarify what it would mean in the medium term and then work out the practicalities of the short term.

DAY 36

The Life Direction Wheel: Core Vision, Values and Goals

LIFE DIRECTION: CORE VISION, VALUES & GOALS			
	KEY QUESTIONS	INGREDIENTS	LONG TERM
VISION	How would you describe your primary purpose in life?	Personal meaning	
VALUES	What are your three most important personal values or golden rules?	Personal principles	
GOALS	What are your top 1-3 goals in life?	Achievements by 'life's end'	

DAY 37

The Life Direction Wheel: Private

	KEY QUESTION	INGREDIENTS	SHORT TERM	MID TERM	LONG TERM
BE	How do you want to develop in your character, inner being or spiritual life?	• Individual fulfilment • Development of potential • Faith			
DO	What do you want to do or achieve in your private life?	• Individual achievements • Sports/leisure/arts • Retirement plan			
LEARN	What do you want to learn or develop skills in?	• Education • Hobbies • Languages • Practical skills			
RESOURCES	What are your plans for your finances and other practical resources?	• Financial goals • Property aspirations • Possessions • Will			

LIFE DIRECTION: PRIVATE

DAY 38

The Life Direction Wheel: Public

LIFE DIRECTION: PUBLIC				
	KEY QUESTION	INGREDIENTS	SHORT TERM	MID TERM	LONG TERM
FAMILY	What are your aspirations for your family life?	• Close friends • Nuclear and extended family			
SOCIAL	What relationships and activities do you want to pursue and enjoy?	• Friendships • Sports or hobby clubs • Cultural activities			
LOCAL	What do you want to do in your local community?	• Neighbourhood activity • Voluntary activity • Faith group			
GLOBAL	What do you want to do in the wider world?	• Charity activities • Politics			

DAY 39

The Life Direction Wheel: Professional

LIFE DIRECTION: PROFESSIONAL				
KEY QUESTIONS	**INGREDIENTS**	**SHORT TERM**	**MID TERM**	**LONG TERM**
CURRENT — What do you want to acheive in your current role?	Desired achievements			
DEVELOP — What relationships and activities do you want to pursue and enjoy?	Desired future skills			
FUTURE — What do you want to do in your local community?	Future opportunities and roles			
LEGACY — What do you want to do in the wider world?	What do you want to pass on?			

DAY 40

Congratulations...

... you have got to the end of this journal. But the journey continues!

Before you close the book and put it on the shelf, take a few minutes to look back at what you have achieved, what you have learned and what has been most useful to you. Over the last eight weeks...

WHAT HAVE YOU DONE LESS OF?

WHAT HAVE YOU DONE MORE OF?

WHAT HAVE YOU DONE DIFFERENTLY?

What three things do you want to remember?

1.

2.

3.

How will you keep them at the forefront of your mind?

Why not write a note to a couple of friends and give them your permission to keep reminding you?

Thanks

"Life is just like an old-time train journey ... delays, side-tracks, smoke, dust, cinders and jolts, interspersed only occasionally by beautiful vistas and thrilling bursts of speed. The trick is to thank the Lord for letting you have the ride."
Jenkin Lloyd Jones

Additionally we have a few other people to thank.

The graphics in *Leaders' Journal* are the work of Bryan Mathers and his team at wapisasa. He has been a perfect collaborator – talented, insightful, challenging, conscientious and charming.

We are also very grateful for the editing skills of Eileen Fursland who thoroughly "got" what we wanted to say, but helped us make it simpler and crisper. Eileen is a delight to work with.

Pulling the content and graphics together into a great format is not an easy task, but Matt Maguire at Candescent Press has yet again done a terrific job.

Leaders' Journal is a crystallisation of some of the things that we have experienced and learnt over many years of working with friends, colleagues and business leaders for which we say a very big thank you. We are particularly grateful to each one who has reviewed *Leaders' Journal* and given us feedback to reach this final volume, especially Jackie Greenway.

Finally, we want to express our great gratitude to our respective families for their tremendous support and surprising interest in what we do.